Chinese Clothing

Cultural China Series

Cultural China Series

Hua Mei

Chinese Clothing

Costumes, Adornments and Culture

Translated by *Yu Hong & Zhang Lei*

CHINA
INTERCONTINENTAL
PRESS

图书在版编目（CIP）数据

中国服饰／华梅著；于红，张蕾译．—北京：五洲传播出版社，
2004.10（2008.5重印）

ISBN 978−7−5085−0612−8

Ⅰ.中... Ⅱ.①华... ②于... ③张... Ⅲ.服饰—文化—中国
—英文 Ⅳ.TU941.12

中国版本图书馆 CIP 数据核字（2004）第 111457 号

中国服饰

撰　　文　华　梅

译　　者　于　红　张　蕾

责任编辑　张　宏

特约编辑　王若行

整体设计　海　洋

出版发行　五洲传播出版社（北京海淀区莲花池东路北小马场6号　邮编:100038）

版式制作　张纪岩

承 印 者　北京华联印刷有限公司

开　　本　720×965毫米　1/16

字　　数　100千字

印　　张　10.5

版　　次　2004 年 10 月第 1 版

印　　次　2008 年 5 月第 3 次印刷

印　　数　8501−13000 册

定　　价　90.00元

Content

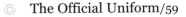

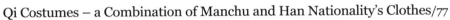

Preface

From the day garments became part of people's lives, they have been given different significance of social status, lifestyle, aesthetics and cultural concepts. Garments have always been the truest and most straightforward reflection of the social and historical scenes of any given time. In this sense, the history of garments is at the same time a vivid history on the development of civilization.

In the Chinese way of describing the necessities of life, clothing ranks at the top of "garments, food, shelter and means of travel." In this country with a long history of garments and ornaments, there is a wealth of archeological findings showing the development of garments, as well as their portrayals in ancient mythology, history books, poems and songs, novels and drama.

The development of the Chinese garments can be traced back to the late Paleolithic age. Archeological findings have shown that approximately 20,000 years ago, the

The Sui Dynasty lady dress, mostly were short jackets with short sleeves and long skirts. They tied the skirts over chest, which made them look very elegant. This way of dressing can be still seen in Korean lady dress. (Painted by Gao Chunming, selected from Lady Garments and Adornments of Chinese Past Dynasties written by Zhou Xun and Gao Chunming)

primitives who lived in the now Zhoukoudian area of Beijing were already wearing personal ornaments, in the form of tiny white stone beads, olive-colored pebbles, animal teeth, clam shells, fish bones and bone tubes, all meticulously perforated. Archeologists have attributed these to be body ornaments. Aesthetics might not have been the only concern when people wore ornaments at that time – ornaments were used as a means of protection against evil. The unearthed bone needles were still intact with oval shaped needle hole, a sign that people at that time were no longer satisfied with utilizing animal and plant materials. They already learned the technology of sewing together animal skin.

Over 1,000 archeological sites of the Neolithic age (6,000 B.C.-2,000 B.C.) have been found in China, geographically covering almost the entire country. The major means of production have transformed from the primitive hunting and fishing to the more stable form of agriculture, while division of labor first appeared in weaving and pottery making. Ancient painted pottery pots from 5,000 years ago were found in Qinghai Province of western China, decorated with dancers imitating the hunting scene. Some dancers wear decorative braids on their heads, while others have ornamental tails on the waist. Some wear full skirts that are rarely seen in traditional Chinese attire, but more similar to the whalebone skirt of the western world. In the neighboring province of Gansu, similar vessels were excavated, with images of people wearing what the later researchers called the "Guankoushan," a typical style found in the early human garments: a piece of textile with a slit or hole in the middle from

A relic of 5600 years history, the colored pottery bottle with a "head" shape bottle neck excavated in Dadiwan, Gansu Province in 1973. The pottery bottle is about 31.8 centimeters high, made of fine red china clay. The facial features of the figure are clear with hair bang and a high nose. The bottle is painted with 3 rows of black color pattern composed of camber line triangle pattern and willow leaf pattern. (Photo by Li Zhanqiang)

The picture shows the colored pottery basin excavated in Tongde County, Qinghai Province in 1975. The pattern is people wearing "distended" skirts dancing hands in hands. This kind of skirt is seldom seen in traditional Chinese garments. (Photo by Li Zhanqiang)

The neck adornments, butterfly shape jade plate and jade excavated in a Neolithic site. (Photo by Li Zhanqiang)

which the head comes through. A rope is tied at the waist, giving the garment a dress-like appearance. Another vessel portrays an image of an attractive young girl, with short bangs on the forehead and long hair in the back. Against the delicate facial features and below the neck a continuous pattern is found with three rows of slanting lines and triangles. It may well have been a lively young girl in a beautiful dress with intricate patterns on the mind of the pottery maker. In addition to the clay vessels, images of primitive Chinese garments were found in rock paintings of the early people wearing ear ornaments. In the Daxi Neolithic site of Wushan, Sichuan, historical artifacts were found including ear ornaments made of jade, ivory and turquoise in round, oblong, trapezoid and even semi-circle shapes.

Along with the establishment of the different social strata, rituals distinguishing the respectable from the humble came into being, leading eventually to the formation of rules and regulations on daily attire. The Chinese rules on garments and ornaments started taking shape in the Zhou Dynasty (1,046 B.C.-256 B.C.), regulating the royalty down to the commoners, and these were recorded in the national decrees and regulations. As early as in the Zhou Dynasty, garments were already classified into sacrificial attire, court attire, army uniform, mourning attire and wedding attire. This tradition was once broken during the Spring and Autumn Period (770 B.C.-476 B.C.) and the Warring States Period (475 B.C.-221 B.C.), in which numerous war lords fought for power and a hundred schools of thoughts contended. As a result, rigid rules on garments and ornaments were replaced by diversity of style, and the aristocratic class went after extravagance.

The rulers of the Han Dynasty (206 B.C.-220 A.D.) used the *Zhou Li* – book on Zhou Dynasty Rituals as the

The picture shows a Tang Dynasty lady with "double-drooping-bun" and wide waist cloth-wrapper. In 8th century, Chinese Tang dresses were spread into Japan and then exerted great influence on Japanese kimono. The kimono styles at that time under the names, such as "Tang grass", "Tang flower" and "Tang brocade" continue to be used even today. (Part of the Tang painting Tuning Qin and Drinking Tea, selected from Lady Garments and Adornments of Chinese Past Dynasties written by Zhou Xun and Gao Chunming)

blueprint and promulgated categorical rules on garments and ornaments. Dress colors were specified into spring green, summer red, autumn yellow and winter black to be in harmony with the seasons and the solar calendar, all in a style of sober simplicity. Women's upper and lower garments became the model for the Han ethnicity of later generations.

The Wei, Jin and Southern and Northern Dynsties (220-589) was a period of ethnic amalgamation with, despite the frequent change in power and incessant wars, ideological diversity, cultural prosperity and significant scientific development. In this period, there was not only the Wei and Jin aristocratic style that the intelligentsia took delight in talking about, but also the shocks and transformations on the traditional Han culture brought about by the northern nomadic tribes when they migrated into the central plains. These ethnic minority people settled down with the Han people. As a result, the way they dressed influenced the Han style, while at the same time it was influenced by the Han style.

When China was reunited in the Sui Dynasty (581-618), the Han dress code was pursued again. In the Tang Dynasty (618-907) that followed, the strong national power and an open social order led to a flourishing of garment and ornament style that is both luxuriant and refreshing, typically with women wearing low cut short shirtdress or narrow-sleeved men's attire. By Song Dynasty (960-1279), the Han women developed the habit of chest-binding, giving popularity to the popular overcoat beizi, whose elegant and simplistic style was favored by women of all ages and all social strata. Yuan Dynasty (1206-1368) was established by the Mongols when they unified China. As Mongols at that time wore maoli or triangular hat, and men commonly wore earrings, the official dress code became a mixture of the inherited Han system with the Mongol elements. When power again changed hands to the Han people, the Ming Dynasty (1368-1644) rulers promulgated decrees prohibiting use of the previous dynasty's Mongol attire, language and surnames, returning to the dress style of the Tang Dynasty. The official uniform of the Ming Dynasty was intent on seeking a sense of dignity and splendor, as shown in the complex forms, styles and dressing rituals of the emperor down to officials of all levels.

More than 200 years of the Qing Dynasty (1644-1911) was a period with the most significant changes in garment style. The Manchu dress style which the rulers tried to force on the Han people was met with strong resistance, but a later compromise by the

At the end of 19th century, sewing machines imported from western countries had already been applied in traditional garments processing industry. (As Beautiful as Evening Primrose painted by Wu Youru)

6 (**left page, left top**) *The traditional image of a peasant wearing a front closure Chinese jacket.* (Photographed in 1950, provided by Xinhua News Agency photo department)

(**left page, right top**) *The students of Beijing University wearing Scotland checked skirts in 1950s.* (Photographed in 1954, provided by Xinhua News Agency photo department)

(**left page, bottom**) *A foreign model wearing a red Chinese cheong-sam in Chinese Garments International Fair.* (Photo by Wu Hong, provided by Imaginechina)

(**right page, left top**) *Fashionable young people on the street.* (Photo by Chen Shu, provided by Imaginechina)

(**right page, right top**) *With more and more international famous clothing brands opening their stores in all parts of China, the Euro-American fashion trends influence more directly the dressing style of Chinese people.* (Provided by Imaginechina)

(**right page, bottom**) *Women of "Long Horn Miao" group in Guizhou Province combed their huge coiled hair.* (Photo by Li Guixuan, provided by image library of Hong Kong *Traveling in China*)

government led to a silent fusion of the two dress styles. The mandarin long gown (*changpao*) and jacket (*magua*) style has become the quintessential Qing style whenever the topic of Qing dress is brought up.

After 1840, China entered the contemporary era. Seaport cities, especially metropolis like Shanghai, led the change towards western style under the influence of the European and American fashion trends. Industrialization in the textile weaving and dyeing in the west brought about the import of low cost materials, gradually replacing domestic materials made in the traditional way. Intricately made and trendy ready-to-wear garments in western style also found their way into the Chinese market, gaining an upper hand over the time-consuming traditional techniques of hand rolling, bordering, inlay and embroidery with its large scale machine operated dress-making.

Looking in retrospect at Chinese garments of the 20th century, we see an array of styles of *qipao*, Cheongsam, the Sun Yat-sen's uniform, student uniform, western suits, hat, silk stockings, high heels, workers' uniform, Lenin jacket, the Russian dress, army style, jacket, bell-bottoms, miniskirts, bikinis, professional attire, punk style and T-shirt, all witnessing the days gone by... The *qipao* dress, now regarded as the typical Chinese dress style, only became popular in the 1920s. Originating in the Manchu women's dress, incorporating techniques of the Han ladies' garments and absorbing styles of the 20th century western dresses, it has now evolved into a major fashion element to be reckoned with in the international fashion industry.

China, as a country made up of 56 ethnic groups that continually influenced each other, has undergone continuous transformation in dress style and customs. The distinction not only existed among dynasties, but also quite pronounced even in different periods within the same dynasty. The overall characteristics of the Chinese garments can be summarized as bright colors, refined artisanship, and ornate details. Diversity in style can be seen among different ethnic groups, living environments, local customs, lifestyles and aesthetic tastes. Chinese folk garments are deeply rooted in the daily life and folk activities of the common people, full of rustic flavor and exuberant with vitality. Many of the folk dresses are still popular today, for example the red velvet flower hair piece, the embroidered keepsakes between lovers, coil hats and raincoats made of natural fiber, not to mention the handmade tiger hats, tiger shoes, pig shoes, cat shoes and the child buttock shields.

The progress of modernization is effacing the ethnic characters of the urban dress style. However in the vast rural areas, especially in areas with a high concentration of ethnic minority people, a wide array of beautiful garments and ornaments are still part of the local lifestyle, offering a unique folk scene together with the local landscape.

Shenyi and Broad Sleeves

The ancient Chinese attached great importance to the upper and lower garments on important ceremonial occasions, believing in its symbolism of the greater order of heaven and earth. At the mean time, one piece style co-existed starting from the *shenyi* of the Warring States Period, and developed into the Han Dynasty robe, the large sleeved *changshan* of the Wei and Jin Period, down to the "qi pao" of the contemporary times, all in the form of a long robe in one piece. Therefore, Chinese garments took the above-mentioned two basic forms.

Shenyi, or deep garment, literally means wrapping the body deep within the clothes. This style is deeply rooted in the traditional mainstream Chinese ethics and morals that forbid the close contact of the male and the female. At that time, even husband and wife were not allowed to share the same bathroom, the same suitcase,

The picture shows the lady dress of the Han Dynasty with overlapping garment pieces and triple collars. The dress body was embroidered with cloud pattern and the sleeves and collar were decorated with brocade edgings that made the wearer look very tall and straight. (Painted by Gao Chunming, selected from Lady Garments and Adornments of Chinese Past Dynasties written by Zhou Xun and Gao Chunming)

10

(Right)The lacquer wood tomb figures excavated in Xinyang in Henan Province. The figures wore long dresses with curved garment pieces, decorative plates and angel sleeves. This type of sleeve was often used afterwards to make the movement of elbow and wrist flexible. Jackets and skirts were their everyday clothes with the skirt pieces overlapping in the behind and decorative jade plates in front of the waist. (Photo by Li Zhanqiang) *(**bottom**) Garment pictures painted by Gao Chunming according to lacquer wooden figurines unearthed in Luoyang, Henan Province.*

or even the same clothing lines. A married woman returning to her mother's home was not permitted to eat at the same table with her brothers. When going out, a woman had to keep herself fully covered. These rules and rituals were recorded in great detail in the Confucian Book of Rites.

The *shenyi* is made up of the upper and lower garment, tailored and made in a unique way. There is a special chapter in the Book of Rites detailing the make of the *shenyi*. It said that in the Warring States Period, the style of the *shenyi* must conform to the rites and rituals, its style fit for the rules with the proper square and round shapes and the perfect balance. It has to be long enough not to expose the skin, but short enough not to drag on the floor. The forepart is elongated into a large triangle, with the part above the waist in straight cut and the part below the waist bias cut, for ease of movement. The underarm section is made for flexible movement of the elbow, therefore the generous length of sleeves reaches the elbow when folded from the fingertips. Moderately formal, the *shenyi* is fit for both men of letters and warriors. It ranks second in ceremonial wear, functional, not wasteful and simple in style. *Shenyi* of this period can be seen in silk paintings unearthed from ancient tombs, as well as on clay and wooden figurines found in the same period, with clear indications of the style, and often even the patterns.

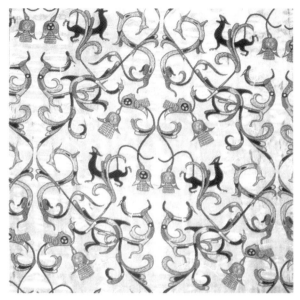

The copy drawing of colored embroidering pattern of dragon, phoenix and tiger. (Selected from *Research on Ancient Chinese Clothes and Adornments* written by Shen Congwen)

A printed Han Dynasty brocade robe. (Painted by Gao Chunming according to the material object excavated in Mawangdui Han Tomb in Changsha, selected from *Lady Garments and Adornments of Chinese Past Dynasties* written by Zhou Xun and Gao Chunming)

Material used for making *shenyi* is mostly linen, except black silk is employed in garments for sacrificial ceremonies. Sometimes a colorful decorative band is added to the edges, or even embellished with embroidered or painted patterns. When *shenyi* is put on, the elongated triangular hem is rolled to the right and then tied right below the waist with a silk ribbon. This ribbon was called *dadai* or *shendai*, on which a decorative piece is attached. Later on leather belt appeared in the garment of the central regions as an influence of nomadic tribes. A belt buckle is normally attached to the leather belt for fastening. Belt buckles are often intricately made, becoming an emerging craft at the Warring States Period. Large belt buckles can be as long as 30 centimeters, whereas the short ones are about 3 centimeters in length. Materials can be stone, bone, wood, gold, jade, copper or iron, with the extravagant ones decorated with gold and silver, carved in patterns or embellished with jade or glass beads.

By Han Dynasty, *shenyi* evolved into what is called the

12

The front piece

The back piece

The sketch drawings of the front and back piece of Shenyi. *(Provided by Zang Yingchun)*

qujupao or curved gown, a long robe with triangular front piece and rounded under hem. At the mean time, the straight gown or *Zhijupao* was also popular, and it was also called *chan* or *yu*. When straight gown first appeared, it was not allowed as ceremonial wear, for wearing out of the house or even for receiving guests at home. In Historical Records, comments are found on the disrespectful nature of wearing Chan and Yu to court. The taboo may have come from the fact that, before Han Dynasty, people in the central plains wore trousers without crotches, only two legs of the trousers that meet at the waist, similar to the Chinese infant pants. For this reason, the wearer may look disgraceful if the outer garment is not properly wrapped to cover the body. When dressing etiquette is discussed in Confucian classics, the outer garment is said not to be lifted even in the hottest days, and the only occasion allowing for lifting the outer garment is when crossing of the river. People of the central plains had to kneel before they sit. There were written rules on not allowing sitting with the two legs forward. This rule has to do with the clothing style of the time, when sitting in the forbidden posture may result in disgrace. Later on, along with the close interaction with the riding nomadic, people of the central plains started to accept trousers with crotches.

Historical evidence, be it Han tomb paintings, painted rocks or bricks, or clay and wooden figurines, all portray people wearing long gowns. This style is found most commonly in men, but sometimes in women as well. The so-called *paofu* refers to long robes with the following features. First of all, it has a lining. Depending on whether it is padded, the garment can be called *jiapao* or *mianpao*. Secondly, it most often comes with generously wide sleeves with cinched wrist. Thirdly, it has low cut cross collars to show the under garment. And fourthly, there is often an embroidered dark band at the collar, the wrists and the front hem, often in Kui (a Chinese mythical animal) or checker patterns. The *paofu* differ in length. Some robes can reach down to the ankles, often worn by men of letters or the elderly, while others are only long enough to cover the knees, worn mostly by warriors or heavy laborers.

Even after *paofu* became the mainstream attire, *shenyi* did not disappear – it remained as in women's garments. First the front lapel elongated and developed into a *shenyi* with wrap-around lapel. As can be seen in the silk painting in the Changsha Mawangdui Tomb of Han Dynasty, the lady in the painting is dressed in a *shenyi* with wrap-around lapel, fully embroidered with dragon and phoenix and already a high achievement in the development of female garments.

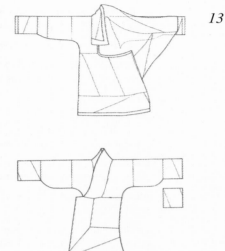

13

The exterior structure sketch drawings of Qujupao. (Selected from Research on Ancient Chinese Clothes and Adornments written by Shen Congwen)

Images of the tomb owner and servants portrayed by brocade paintings of Han Tomb of Mawangdui in Changsha, Hunan Province. (Selected from Research on Ancient Chinese Clothes and Adornments written by Shen Congwen)

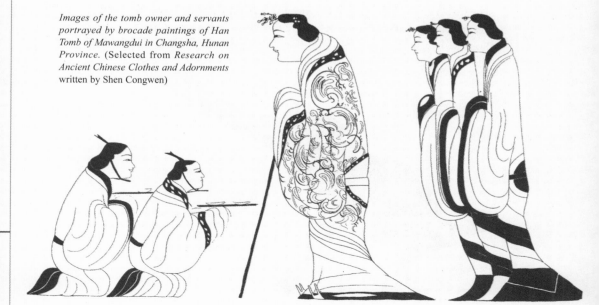

14

By the Wei, Jin and Southern and Northern Dynasties (220-589), style of *paofu* evolved into loose-fitting garments with open sleeves (as opposed to cinched sleeves of the previous dynasties). These were called *bao yi bo dai* or loose robes with long ribbons, exemplifying the carefree style of the wearer. Men's long robes became increasingly casual and simple, while women's long robes became more elaborate and complex. Typical women's garments were well exemplified in the painting of the Gu Kaizhi (circa. 345-409), the great painter of the time. Women wore dresses with decorative cloth on the lower hems of their dresses. These pieces were triangular, and hung like banners with rolled edges and embroidered decorative patterns. When the top of the lapel is wrapped up, these triangles create a layered effect and lend rhythm to the women's movement. Wide sleeves and long hemline, together with the long silk ribbons tying the decorative cloth around the waist, add to the grace of the wearer.

There are both similarities and differences between *shenyi* and *paofu*. They are both one-piece gowns but *shenyi* died out while *paofu* survived up until the present day. Even today in the 21st century, the mere mention of the *changpao* will bring up an image of a straight gown with side opening under the right arm, its simplicity in style enhanced by the elaboration of weaving and embroidery.

The style of *paofu* continually evolved in each dynasty. The Han Dynasty *shenyi* with wide sleeves, the Tang Dynasty round collar gown and the Ming Dynasty straight gown are all typical wide *changpao*s, mainly preferred by the intelligentsia and the ruling class. Time went by, and the *changpao* became a typical garment for those with leisure, as well as a traditional garment of the Han people.

The belt hook is a kind of hanging hook carried at the one end of the leather belt in ancient China. As early as the early years of the Spring and Autumn Period, there were belt hooks on leather belts. (Photo by Li Zhanqiang)

Royal Ceremonial Wear

The *mianfu* and the dragon robe are typical garments for ancient Chinese emperors. They serve as a micro cosmos that exemplify the unique Chinese aesthetic and sense of the universe.

In Chinese history there is a story of "Dressed with yellow robe" that occurred in 959 A.D. One year after a young emperor took over the throne at the death of his father, the old emperor, a general was dressed with the royal yellow robe by his supporters and made emperor. That was the beginning of the Song Dynasty. But why does the "yellow robe" represent the emperor? It all started in the Han Dynasty.

The Chinese theories of the Yin and Yang and of the Five Elements all try to explain the interdependence and mutual rejection of gold, wood, water, fire and earth. White represents gold; green represents wood; black represents water; and yellow represents earth. In Zhou Dynasty, red was regarded as the superior

A queen of the Five Dynasties Period wearing a long robe with wide sleeves and a phoenix crown. (Painted by Gao Chunming, selected from Lady Garments and Adornments of Chinese Past Dynasties written by Zhou Xun and Gao Chunming)

16

A drawing of Han Emperor's Mianfu.
(Painted by Gao Chunming)

A Song Dynasty emperor wearing a futou
hat and a round neck robe. (Painted by Hua
Mei according to the *Portraits of Emperors
and Queens of Past Dynasties* stored in the
Nanxun Palace)

color for garments, but by Qin Dynasty (221 B.C.-206 B.C.) black ranked highest among all garment colors. All officials followed suit and wore black as much as they could. When Han Dynasty replaced Qin, yellow was promoted to the highest place, favored by the emperors of the time. By Tang Dynasty the court made it official that no one, except the emperor, had the right to wear yellow. This rule was passed all the way down to the Qing Dynasty. It was said that when the 11-year old Pu Yi (1906-1967), the last emperor, saw his 8-year old cousin wearing yellow silk as his clothes lining, he grabbed the sleeve and said: "How dare you use yellow!" The status of the color yellow was apparently supreme in their heart.

In ancient Chinese society, it was all strictly specified which class should wear what on what occasions. What the emperor wore on important occasions had a special name: *mianfu.*

Mianfu is a set of garments including the *mianguan,* a crown with a board that leans forward, as if the emperor is bowing to his subjects in full respect and concern. Chains of beads hang at front and back, normally twelve chains each, but also in numbers of nine, seven, five or three, depending on the importance of the occasion and the difference in ranks. The jade beads are threaded with silk, ranging from nine to twelve in number. Hairpins are used to fasten the crown to the hair, and two small beads hang above the ears of the wearer, reminding him to listen with discretion. This, like the board in front of the crown, has important political significance.

The upper garment of emperors is normally black while the lower garment is normally crimson. They symbolize the order of heaven and earth and should

Portraits of an emperor and a queen of the Qing Dynasty. (Part of *Portraits of Emperors and Queens of the Qing Dynasty* colleted by Beijing Palace Museum)

never be confused. Dragon is the dominant pattern embroidered on the emperors clothing, although another 12 kinds of decoration can be seen as well, including symbolic animals, or natural scenes with sun and moon. These patterns are allowed on the lords as well, but they differ in complexity according to different ranks and importance of the occasion.

Mianfu with upper and lower garments are fastened with a belt, under which a decorative piece called *bixi* or knee covering hangs down. This piece of decorative cloth originated in the days when people were wearing animal skins, used primarily for covering the abdomen and the genitals. This part of clothing remained until later years, becoming an important component of the ceremonial wear. Even later, the *bixi* became the protector of the royal dignity. The emperor's *bixi* is pure red in color.

Shoes to go with the *mianfu* are made of silk with double-layered wooden soles. Another kind exists that uses flax or animal skin as the sole depending on the season. By order of importance, the emperor wore red, white or black shoes on different occasions.

The most outstanding feature of the Chinese royal attire is the embroidered dragon. In Ming and Qing Dynasties, the robe had to have nine dragons embroidered, on front and back of the two shoulders and two sleeves, as well as inside the front lapel, displaying the royal prominence bestowed by the gods.

An imperial waistcoat of Qing Dynasty queen. (Colleted by Beijing Palace Museum)

Introduction of Ethnic Minority Styles

In as early as the Warring States Period, the sixth emperor of Zhao already realized that although the Zhao army had better weapons, the long robes worn by generals and warriors were too cumbersome for an army, especially when they had to drag their armors and supplies around. They had tens of thousands of soldiers, but few riders flexible to make a quick attack. He went against all objections and advocated for change towards the Hu or western minority clothing style of the nomadic riders. The Zhao soldiers wore shorter robes and trousers and soon became a better army. Economic development followed.

Moreover, this style that was once frowned upon and rejected became the daily wear of the common folks by Wei, Jin and Southern and Western Dynasties in the central plains. One reason for this change, unfortunately, was the frequent migration of the people to run away from the incessant wars and chaos. This

A pottery tomb figure wearing Kuzhe. (Photo by Li Zhanqiang)

process also helped the exchange of garment culture.

Kuzhe and *liangdang* are the typical "Hu" or minority wear of that time. It is not hard to see that both styles are fit for riding and for life in the cold climate.

The so-called *kuzhe* is a style with separate upper and lower garments. The upper garment looks like a short robe with wide sleeves, a central China adaptation to the original narrow sleeves fit for riding and herding animals. What also changed was the closure of the robe, which moved from left to right. Interestingly, people of central China called the northwestern people "people with left closure." The robes at this time were shortened significantly, and varied in style. Historical materials show a number of styles of these upper garments in Wei, Jin, Southern

Song Dynasty riders of North China wearing fur hats, racoon dog fur sleeves and carrying marten fur arrow bags. (Selected from *Research on Ancient Chinese Clothes and Adornments* written by Shen Congwen)

and Northern Dynasties, which had left, right and middle closure, or even swallowtails at the front hem. A set of these garments makes the wearer sharp and agile, as is frequently seen in clay burial figurines in the Southern Dynasty.

The lower garment of the *kuzhe* is a pair of trousers with closed crotch. Initially these trousers were close fitting, showing off slender legs that could freely move around. When this style appeared in central China, especially when some officials wore them in court, the conservatives questioned the appropriateness of the two thin legs that cried out rebellion against the loose fitting traditional ceremonial wear. Widening the legs was a compromise, so that the pants still appeared similar to the traditional robe. When walking about, these pants were more flexible and convenient than the robe. To avoid being caught in thorns or dragged in mud, someone came up with a brilliant idea of lifting the trouser legs and tying them up just below knee-level. This kind of pants can be frequently seen in the Southern Dynasty's burial figurines and brick paintings. In appearance, they are quite similar to the bell bottomed pants in the modern days, but in reality, they are only similar in profile, not in construction.

Liangdang or double-layered suit is another style typical of this period, and it came from the northwest into central China. It was no more than a vest, which can be seen in many burial pieces of that time. Judging from clay figurines and wall paintings in tombs, the

Kuzhe. (Painted by Zhou Xun, selected from *Lady Garments and Adornments of Chinese Past Dynasties* written by Zhou Xun and Gao Chunming)

vest was in two separate pieces fastened on the shoulders and under the arms. There were also *liangdang*s worn inside in materials of leather or cotton, lined or unlined, close or loose fitting. The name has changed over the years but the style remained.

The above mention garments were all the rage at that time for both women and men. The separate piece style has always been the prototype of the Chinese people, but modifications were made due to the exchange and fusion of different garment cultures.

The Warring States Period (475 B.C.–221 B.C.) bronze human figures wearing silk girdles, embroidered short robes and short swords. (Excavated in Changzhi, Shanxi Province) These are palinspastic maps of their dresses. (Selected from Research on Ancient Chinese Clothes and Adornments *written by Shen Congwen)*

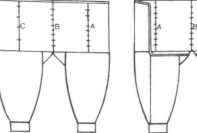

The structural sketch map for men's trousers in the Warring States Period. (Selected from Research on Ancient Chinese Clothes and Adornments *written by Shen Congwen)*

The Elegant Wei and Jin Period

In China's political history, the Wei and Jin Period was a period of volatility, which spanned over 200 years. Frequent changes in political power and incessant wars added to the suffering of the people, who were already devastated by natural disasters and plagues. The once dominant laws and orders collapsed. So did the once unchallenged power of Confucianism. At the meantime, the philosophy of Lao Zi and Zhuang Zi became popular; Buddhist scripture was translated; Daoism developed; and humanitarian ideology emerged among the aristocrats. The aristocratic descendants aspired individualism and led the trend in all aspects of social life. This rank of "cultural elite" was engaged in making friends, making social

The picture shows a lady in the Wei & Jin Dynasty wearing a long robe with wide sleeves and overlapping hems, and scorpion tail shape hairstyle on temples, a kind of ancient hairstyle in the Warring States Period and Western Han Dynasty. (Painted by Zhou Xun, selected from *Lady Garments and Adornments of Chinese Past Dynasties* written by Zhou Xun and Gao Chunming)

24

commentaries and controlling public opinions. Their behavior posed a threat to the conservative and the imperial power, which tried to crush them by force.

It is not unfitting to say that the life threatening danger and distress was unsurpassed in the Wei and Jin Dynasties. However, another typical image of the Wei and Jin literati was on that indulgence in drinking, merry making, and talking of metaphysics. The treacherous nature of politics forced these scholars to seek comfort and relief in these aspects. Facing the hypocrisy and constraint of traditional orders, they

The picture shows clothes and adornments for noble people in the Wei & Jin Dynasty. The noble man dress image wearing a Liang hat in the left lower picture was followed by Japanese imperial men's full dress. (Painted according to the frescos in Liaoyang ancient tomb in Liaoning Province, selected from *Research on Ancient Chinese Clothes and Adornments* written by Shen Congwen)

preferred a life of truth and freedom. They sought the carefree lifestyle, the maintenance of good health or indulgence in earthly pleasures. These aristocrats changed significantly in aesthetic taste and behavior, intentionally breaking away from traditional morality in their daily life. Some dressed themselves in free and casual elegance while the rest went to both extremes, sloppy or meticulous.

In this period, people were divided into nine classes by their ranks in court or their property. A clear-cut line was drawn to separate these classes, who may never marry each other. Not only the rich used every opportunity of weddings and funerals to show off their wealth, but the commoners also followed suit. There was an story in *Shi-shuo Hsin-yu* (A New Account of Tales of the World) that a scholar Ruan Ji (210-263) and his niece Ruan Xian, lived south of the road while some better-off Ruans lived north of the road. Every year on July the 7th of the lunar calendar, the northern Ruans took out their clothing to be aired under the sun, showing off their silks and brocades. In response to this Ruan Ji took out his shoddy underwear made of coarse homespun cloth and sunned it on a bamboo pole. This behavior itself was sarcasm against the showing off and the Confucian formalities with clothes.

The "Seven Gentlemen of the Bamboo Forest" refers to the seven gentlemen of the Wei and Jin Period, including Ruan Ji and Ruan Xian. Today we can still see on wall paintings how they once dressed – the front of the garment dragging to the floor, exposing the chest, arms, shins and feet. This is a rare scene among the literati of the Chinese feudal society, because only the lower class exposed their arms and legs. Moreover, their characters were no less defiant than their clothes.

25

The cage hat was popular in wide areas in middle land of China and was a major hat style in the Northern Dynasty. The picture shows a kind of exquisite white lacquer gauze hat for the noble men in the Northern Dynasty. (Selected from Research on Ancient Chinese Clothes and Adornments written by Shen Congwen)

In paintings, Liu Ling, Ji Kang and Wang Rong of the "seven gentlemen" had their hair done in children's buns, cynical of all the tradition and customs of the world.

As far as Chinese folk garments are concerned, the taste of the literati significantly expanded the aesthetics of ancient China. The Chinese classical sense of beauty started out as something quite simple: soft hands and supple skin, sweet smile and beautiful eyes formed the ideal beauty of the Spring and Autumn Period, praising the unpretentious and natural beauty. By the Wei and Jin Period, descriptions of female beauty moved on to include the hairstyle, the dresses and the ornaments. The more sophisticated aesthetics of the Wei and Jin Period brought about great progress in dress and ornaments.

In the Wei and Jin Period, especially during the Eastern Jin Period (317-420), the aristocratic women went after an uninhibited life style along with the collapse of the Eastern Han feudal ethical code. These women looked down upon the role society imposed on them, and immersed themselves in socializing, sightseeing,

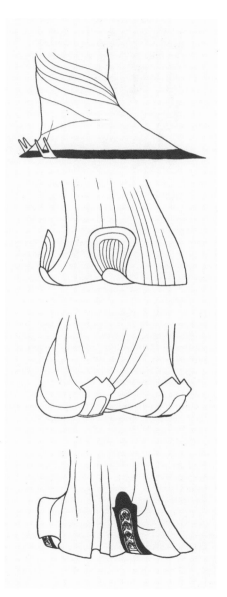

(**left page**) *The picture shows a Southern Dynasty lady wearing double-bun, a long robe with wide sleeves and low collar and shoes with high shoe tips.* (Painted by Gao Chunming, selected from *Lady Garments and Adornments of Chinese Past Dynasties* written by Zhou Xun and Gao Chunming)
(**right page**) *The shoe tip styles of, from top down, Han Dynasty, Southern and Northern Dynasties, Sui Dynasty and Tang Dynasty.* (Selected from *Research on Ancient Chinese Clothes and Adornments* written by Shen Congwen)

28

The Tang Dynasty painting Eremites *shows the image of light-hearted and unrestrained scholars in the Wei & Jin Dynasty.* (Provided by Hua Mei)

and studies of art, literature and metaphysics, completely defying the feudalistic "virtues" of women. This carefree life style brought about the development of women's garments in the direction of extravagant and ornate beauty. Wide sleeves and long robes, flying ribbons and floating skirts, elegant and majestic hair ornaments – all these became the trend of Wei and Jin garments.

The Thousand Faces of the Tang Costume

In terms of cultural and economic development of the feudal society, the Tang Dynasty in China was doubtless a peak in the development of human civilization. The Tang government not only opened up the country to the outside world, allowing foreigners to do business and come to study, but went so far as to allowing them in exams for selection of government officials. It was tolerant, and often appreciative, of religions, art and culture from the outside world. Chang'an, the Tang capital, therefore became the center of exchange among different cultures. What is worth special mention is that women of the Tang Dynasty did not have to abide by the traditional dress code, but were allowed to expose their arms and back when they dressed, or wear dresses absorbing elements from other cultures. They could wear men's riding garments if

Tang Dynasty clothes were very diverse and could be divided into three types: short coats or jackets with tight sleeves and long skirts, hufu, and women wearing men's clothes. The picture shows a noble lady wearing a high bun, a "half arm", a long skirt and a piece of wrapping brocade. (Painted by Zhou Xun, selected from Lady Garments and Adornments of Chinese Past Dynasties written by Zhou Xun and Gao Chunming)

Noble women and footmen riding horses with fancy saddles in the first half of 8th century. (Copied according to Tang Dynasty painting Huo Kingdom Ladies Going on a Tour, selected from *Research on Ancient Chinese Clothes and Adornments* written by Shen Congwen)

they liked, and enjoyed right to choose their own spouse or to divorce him. Materialistic abundance and a relatively relaxed social atmosphere gave Tang Dynasty the unprecedented opportunity to develop culturally, reaching its height in poetry, painting, music and dance. Based on the development in textiles in the Sui Dynasty, and progress made in silk reeling and dyeing techniques, the variety, quality and quantity of textile materials reached unprecedented height, and the variety of dress styles became the trend of the time.

The most outstanding garments in this great period of prosperity were women's dresses, complimented by elaborate hairstyles, ornaments and face makeup. The Tang women dressed in sets of garments, each set a unique image in itself. People no longer dressed by their whims, but played up the full beauty of their garment based on their social background. Each matching set of garments had its own unique character, as well as a deep cultural grounding. In general, the Tang women's dresses can be classified into three categories: the *hufu*, or alien dress that came from the Silk Road, the traditional *ruqun* or double layered or padded short jacket that was typical of central China, as well as the full set of male garments that broke the tradition of the Confucian formalities.

Let's first talk about the *ruqun*, which is made up of the top jacket and long gown and a skirt on the bottom. The Tang women inherited this traditional style and developed it further, opening up the collar as far as exposing the cleavage between the breasts. This was unheard of and unimaginable in the previous dynasties, in which women had to cover their entire body according to the Confucian classics. But the new style was soon embraced by the open-minded aristocratic women of the Tang Dynasty.

Zhang Xuan, a woman painter of the Tang Dynasty, and Zhou Fang, another famous painter, were particularly good at portraying opulent women in elaborate dresses. Zhou Fang, in his painting *Lady with the Flower in the Hair*, portrayed a beauty with a long gown lightly covering the breasts, revealing soft and supple shoulders under a silk cape.

The Tang aesthetics was that of suppleness and opulence, like peonies in flowers, men and women with short necks and shoulders, and horses with small head, thick neck and a large backside. In Tang paintings, women tried to show their suppleness by pleating their skirts in accordion form, and raised the waist all the way up to under the armpits, so that the waistline was barrel shaped to show a full and round body contour.

Descriptions of the Tang dresses were

A screen paining drawn by a Japanese painter with the theme of a Chinese lady of the Tang Dynasty. The painting shows the influence that the Tang clothes had on Japanese dressing image.

Hu *clothes and hats were popular in Wuzetian Period (684-704) and their major features were long robes with tight sleeves and turn-up collars and soft brocade boots.* (These three human figure images were copied according to the frescos excavated in Weixiang Tomb in Xi'an, Shaanxi Province, selected from *Research on Ancient Chinese Clothes and Adornments* written by Shen Congwen)

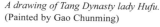
32

found in a vast array of poems, both in terms of style and color. A vast array of colors was found in the poems, because there was no official decree on what color was or was not appropriate. Personal preference was all that mattered, be it deep red, apricot yellow, deep violet, ultramarine, sap green or turmeric. Pomegranate red was popular for the longest time. In poems by Li Bai, Du Fu and Bai Juyi, the most outstanding poets of the time, lady in pomegranate skirt was an enduring image of beauty. *Song of May in Yanjing* had an interesting account of the pomegranate-red skirt. It was so popular that in the season when pomegranate blossoms colored the city in red, every household was buying the flower to dye the dresses of their girls. Turmeric skirt was also colored with vegetable dye. The skirt had the beauty of the turmeric color as well as the fragrance that stayed in the skirt. A feather skirt worn by a princess in the mid Tang Dynasty was woven with feathers from a hundred birds. An outstanding piece of work in the history of Chinese costume and textiles, the skirt had varying colors in daytime and at night, under sunlight and under night light, held upright and upside-down. Moreover, images of birds were woven all over the skirt, coming to life in the play of light.

There is more to the woman's *ruqun* than the upper and lower garment. The dress had many matching accessories and ornaments to go with it, including a short sleeve shirt called *banbi* or half-arm, worn outside of the long sleeve jacket, unlike what we do now in summertime. Named a half-arm because the length of the sleeve was somewhere between the vest and the long sleeve, it functioned just like a vest.

The Tang women favored the *pizi* or cape, or as an

A drawing of Tang Dynasty lady Hufu.
(Painted by Gao Chunming)

alternative, a large piece of silk draped over the arms. The difference is that the cape was wide and short, draped over one shoulder of the wearer. The cape is seen on many clay burial figurines unearthed from Tang tombs. There was a story that the Imperial Concubine Yang Yuhuan had her cape blown away onto someone's hat during a royal banquet. Judging from this story the cape must have been light and thin, although we cannot exclude the possibility that heavier capes made from wool were used in winter to shield the body from the cold wind. The *pibo*, however, is much longer and narrower. Draped over the shoulder from back to front, it is what we normally call the "ribbon" – a beautiful piece rarely forgotten in classic Chinese paintings.

Footwear to go with *ruqun* includes brocade shoes with tipped-up "phoenix head" toes, and shoes made with flax or cattail stems, all very light and delicate. In addition to images in classic paintings, we are able to

Tang Dynasty men's clothes were mainly round neck robes. The robes were used widely by emperors and officials and for occasions like visiting and banqueting and even for attending court. (Part of the Song painting Men of Tang Dynasty Riding Horses, *provided by Hua Mei)*

The chart of the make-up order for Tang Dynasty women.

A facial make-up of Tang women. (Drawn by Gao Chunming)

The 1st step	The 2nd step	The 3rd step	The 4th step
Put powder	Rouge	Darken the eyebrow	Decorate fore-head with a yellow crescent

The 5th step	The 6th step	The 7th step
Put ornament on the cheek	Paint "red slant"	Put lipstick

see real pieces unearthed in Xinjiang and other places.

When wearing the *ruqun*, the Tang women rarely wore hats. Sometimes they wore decorative flower crowns, but when out, they often covered their faces with a veil. This kind of veil hat became the trend in the early Tang Dynasty, but by mid-Tang Dynasty many no longer bothered to wear it, but chose to show their hair buns when they were out riding. There was a large variety of hairstyles at that time, all competing for opulence and extravagance, including over 30 kinds of tall buns, double buns, and downward buns, most of which named after their shapes. Some of these hairstyles came from ethnic minority groups. A full range of ornamental objects was used on the buns, including gold hairpins, jade ornaments, as well as fresh or silk flowers. This is often seen in Tang paintings, as well as in artifacts unearthed in ancient tombs.

Although facial makeup was not invented by the Tang women, they were quite elaborate and extravagant. They not only powdered their faces, darkened their eyebrows, rouged their cheeks or put on lipsticks. These women also decorated their foreheads with a yellow crescent, which was said to be an imitation of the northwestern ethnic minorities. Eyebrows were painted in different shapes. It was said that the Xuanzong Emperor asked his court painter to record the ten eyebrow styles, which all had different names, such as the "mandarin duck," the "small peak," the "drooping pearl," and the "dark fog." The commoners had their own trendy brow styles as well. Moreover, decorative designs are put between the eyebrows as a finishing touch, made with feathers, seashells, fish bones, pure gold, or just painted on. At

The facial make-up sketch drawings for different periods in the Tang Dynasty. (Provided by Hua Mei)

36

the tip of each eyebrow there is a "red slant." Lips are painted into the trendiest shapes of the time, complimented by an artificial red dimple about one centimeter from each side of the lips. At the most prosperous time of the Tang Dynasty, these dimples went so far as to reach the two sides of the nose, in shapes of coins, peaches, birds and flowers. We can see this kind of dimples in the Dunhuang Grottos of the Five Dynasties.

These facial makeup styles were not the invention of the Tang Dynasty, but rather had their roots in the previous dynasties. For example, the Huadian or forehead decoration was said to have originated in the Southern Dynasty, when the Shouyang Princess was taking a walk in the palace in early spring and a light breeze brought a plum blossom onto her forehead. The plum blossom for some reason could not be washed off or removed in any way. Fortunately, it looked beautiful on her, and all of a sudden became all the rage among the girls of the commoners. It is therefore called the "Shouyang makeup" or the "plum blossom makeup." This makeup was popular among the women for a long time in the Tang and Song Dynasties. As for the "red slant," it was said that Cao Pi, Weiwen Emperor of the Three Kingdoms Period, had a favorite

A piece of silk painting excavated from Scripture Hidden Cave in Dunhuang. (9th century)

The evolution chart of eyebrow painting styles for Tang women.

(Drawn by Gao Chunming)

	Zhenguan Period (627-649)
	The 1st year of Linde Period (664)
	The 1st year of Zongzhang Period (668)
	The 4th year of Chuigong Period (688)
	The 1st year of Ruyi Period (692)
	The 1st year of Wansui Dengdui Period (696)
	The 2nd year of Chang'an Period (702)
	The 2nd year of Shenlong Period (706)
	The 1st year of Jingyun Period (710)
	The 2nd year of Xiantian Period — The 2nd year of Kaiyuan Period (713-714)
	The 3rd year of Tianbao Period (744)
	The 11th year of Tianbao Period (after 752)
	About the 1st year of Tianbao-Yuanhe Period (about 742-806)
	About the last year of Zhenyuan Period (about 803)
	Late Tang Dynasty (about 828-907)
	Late Tang Dynasty (about 828-907)

imperial concubine named Xue Yelai. One night when Cao Pi was reading, Xue Yelai came by and accidentally hurt her temple on the crystal screen. When the wound healed, the scar remained, as did the love of the emperor. All girls in court tried to imitate her, painting a red mark on both sides of the face. This kind of makeup was initially called the "morning sun makeup," as the color was close to the rosy dawn. It was later called the "red slant".

Concerning the eyebrows, it was said in a Song Dynasty history book that the Yang Emperor of the Sui Dynasty noticed a girl with painted long eyebrows among thousands of beautiful women in a boat ride in the dragon and phoenix shaped boats.

When finally the Tang women decided there was no space left for painting on the face, they all of a sudden changed their makeup style. According to history book, after the mid-Tang Dynasty, the trend became not wearing power or rouge on the face. The only makeup that remained was the black lipstick. It was called the "weeping makeup" or "tears makeup".

Compared with the gorgeous dress of the *ruqun*, a full set of men's

riding attire on women had its own unique flavor. The typical men's wear in the Tang Dynasty included the *futou* or *turban*, round collar jacket and gown, belt on the waist and dark leather boots. Women dressed like this look sharp, unrestrained yet elegant. Although in Confucian teachings long ago it was said that men and women should never cross-dress, women in men's dressed are frequently seen in Tang paintings and in the Dunhuang Grottos. Historical records on Tang garments all told us that in those days, Tang women often wore full sets of men's clothes including boots, gowns, horsewhips and hats. Aristocrats, commoners, at home, or going out, many women dressed like this in those days. It is not hard to imagine that Tang was a rather open society as far as women are concerned.

Such is the extravagance of the Tang garments. Nowadays people call any front closure Chinese jacket the "Tang costume," as a general term for addressing all traditional Chinese garments. However, the term is used only because people today take pride in those prosperous days. In reality, the modern "Tang costumes" have far less of the luster, extravagance and vitality compared to the real thing. The grandeur of the metropolis where all nations came to admire made the Tang Dynasty nothing short of the kingdom of garments.

Copy part of Chao Yuan Xian Zhang, Music Section.
(Selected from *Research on Ancient Chinese Clothes and Adornments* written by Shen Congwen)

Silk, the Silk Road and the Art of Embroidery

As we all know, silk is the invention of China, and for a long period of time, China was the only country producing and using silk.

In Chinese legend, Lei Zu, the royal concubine of the Yellow Emperor, was the first one to raise silkworms and make silk. The ancient Chinese emperors all worshipped her as the silkworm goddess. Archaeological data shows that the Chinese started using silk from silkworm even earlier than the days of Leizu. In the Warring States Period, Xun Zi (circa. 313-238 B.C.) already wrote *Praise to the Silkworm*, which told the story of the "horse-head girl." One day a girl's father was abducted by his neighbor, and only his horse remained. The girl's mother promised that whoever took the father back home would get to marry the young girl. Hearing this promise, the girl ran away, and returned with the man of the household. The mother, however, forgot about her promise. The sad

A huihu princess wearing huihu clothes and a huihu hair bun shown in the frescos in Yulin Caves in Anxi, Gansu Province. (Copied by Zhang Daqian, provided by Hua Mei)

horse refused to eat, crying all day. Finding out about the cause of all this, the angry father killed the horse and left the skin under the sun. One day the girl was walking by. The horse skin wrapped her up and brought her up the mulberry tree. They turned into a silkworm, and ever since that day the girl had been worshipped as the silkworm goddess. The influence of the silkworm goddess went as far as Southeast Asia and Japan, where the "horse-head girl" is still worshipped until the present day.

In addition to anecdotes and fairy tales, there are even more accurate proof on the early use of silk. In 1958 at the Liangzhu historical site located in now what is Yuhang of Zhejiang Province, some silk textiles were excavated made 4,700 years ago, including silk threads, silk ribbons, silk strings, and pieces of silk, all held in the basket. These were made from silk of home raised silkworm according to expert opinion. Although these historical relics have been carbonized, the warps and wefts were still quite clear. The silk ribbons were made from 16 strands of thick and thin silk threads, 5 millimeter in width. The threads were 3 mm in cast width, and made with three strands of silk, a clear sign that the silk textile of that time had reached some degree of sophistication.

As early as 3000 years ago, the Shang Dynasty bone and tortoise shell inscriptions already had characters meaning silkworm, mulberry tree, silk, and gauze. It is apparent that silk was already playing an important role in the production of that time.

In the Yin Ruins of Anyang, Henan Province, the bronze vessels and weapons at the same time of the bone and tortoise shell inscriptions all had textures of textiles, indicating that by Shang Dynasty there was already multi-color brocade with complicated patterns. In 1959, the Meiyan Site of Wujiang, Jiangsu Province unearthed some black pottery with patterns of silkworm, realistically rendered in great

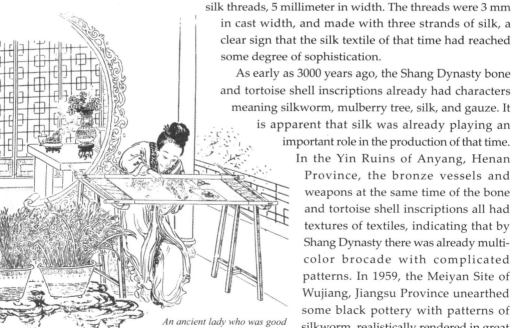

An ancient lady who was good at embroidery. (Part of *Cai Nu Luo*, painted by Wu Youru)

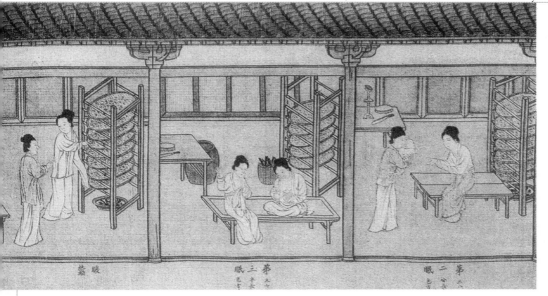

Part of the Song Dynasty silk scroll Silkworm Breeding. *The painting shows the silkworm breeding scenes in Jiangsu and Zhejiang Provinces.* (Provided by Wang Shucun)

familiarity. In *Shangshu* (Book of Historical Records), a Confucian classic that recorded important information on the language, writing, literature, philosophy, aesthetics, mythology and social life of ancient China, there were clear record of silk as articles of tribute, in all colors and forms.

In the Spring and Autumn and the Warring States Periods, agricultural development reached a new height. One important feature of the economy at that time was the division of labor between men and women, who were engaged separately in farming and weaving. Planting of mulberry trees and weaving of textiles were typical scenes of economic activity of that time. Technology of silk reeling was already very developed, as the silk threads spun from this silk were as even and refined as in the modern day. By Han Dynasty, the art of spinning and weaving moved further forward. Brocade excavated from the western Han Dynasty Tomb of Mawangdui in Changsha of Hunan Province in 1972 had yarns made from 4 or 5 strands of thread, and each thread was spun from 14 or 15 pieces of fibers. That is to say that each yarn is made up of 54 pieces of fiber. High development in spinning pushed further forward the art of dyeing and embroidery, giving the finished product added beauty and vivid expression.

In the profound cultural heritage, the unique beauty of silk has become a symbol of eastern aesthetics. It is can be said that because of silk, Chinese garments had the

The Boluo Lake, located besides the Silk Road in 50 kms northwest of Dunhuang, originally a lake of vast expanse of water, it changed into a small piece of unlinked swampland and barren lakebed. (Provided by Imaginechina)

graceful flow, and the figures in classic Chinese paintings had the graceful style we now so admire.

Judging from the evolution of the bronze culture, cultural exchange between China and countries in central and western Asia started in as early as 2000 B.C. In the long journey of history, it was the communication and exchange among different peoples and regions that brought about the splendid variety of the garments. And one cannot talk about cultural exchange without mention of the Silk Road, and the irreplaceable role it played.

From the 5th Century B.C., Chinese textiles started to travel to the west. The exquisite beauty of silk was hailed as something from heaven. Greeks and the Romans called the China "Serica," and the Chinese people were called "Seris," both of which originated from the word "Serge" or silk. According to a western historical book, Caesar (100-44 B.C.) wore a silk robe to watch a play, and all audiences shifted their attention from the play to the silk robe. Chinese silk was introduced to India in very early days, because historical books had very early record of "reams of silk from China." As early as in the 2nd Century A.D., there was already law in India prohibiting the stealing of silk.

In 138 B.C. and 119 B.C., Emperor Wu of Han twice sent his envoy Zhang Qian to travel to the Western Regions, taking along a large quantity of silk, porcelain and other products from central China. Along this road, they used silk textiles as gifts or articles in exchange for food. At the meantime, these countries along the road gave woolen fabrics and spices to China in return. Ever since then, Chinese silk began to be regularly transported along this route to many parts of the world. From Han to Tang Dynasties, ceaseless camel bells marked the prosperity of the "Silk Road."

In as early as the age of the Roman Empires, silk was brought into the Roman market through Persia, leading to a great trade surplus. In the 3rd Century A.D., silk in Rome was once as valuable as gold, so expensive that Emperor Iulianus no longer wore silk, and prohibited his wife from wearing silk. In the 4th Century, the improved economic condition brought about a renewed trend of wearing silk in Constantinople, spreading all the way down to the lower classes.

When the Byzantine emperor Justinian was in reign, the art of raising silkworms was introduced into the country. By the mid of the 6th Century A.D., the entire process of silk making, from the production of raw material to the weaving of finished product, finally took root in East Roman Empire.

What we usually call the Silk Road started from Chang'an (today's Xi'an), then capital of the Western Han, and extended all the way to the Baltic Sea. As one end of the road extended towards the west, the other end extended to Japan. In 107 A.D., the Japanese emperor sent a delegation of 160 people to China, learning the art of embroidery, sewing, and the weaving of brocade. After the delegation returned to Japan, the members reported to the

A modern Uygur lady in Talimu Basin, Xinjiang Autonomous Region wearing locally produced "Aidelice" Silk. (Photo by Song Shijing, provided by image library of Hong Kong *Traveling in China*)

Emperor on what they had seen, and presented the silk and brocade they had brought back. In over 100 years since that time, many artisans from Japan were sent to China to learn specific crafts, while China sent its weavers to Japan, bringing about significant progress in ancient Japan in the art of silk. In 457 A.D., Emperor Yuryaku Tenno was extremely enthusiastic about the craft of textile and embroidery, so he ordered his royal concubines to raise silkworm so that he could realize his dream of Japan as the "kingdom of garments." At his deathbed, he expressed his sorrow in not seeing enough beautiful garments in the field. In the 7th and 8th centuries, the ceremonial gown of the Japanese emperor had patterns of the sun, the moon, the star, the mountain, the dragon, the pheasant and the fire embroidered over red silk, quite similar to what was being worn by Chinese emperors.

In *Lectures on the Art of Clothing* published in Japan, garments in the Japanese Asuka Times (552-645), Nara Times (673-794) and the early Heian Times (794-1192) were called the age of Sui and Tang imitations. Japanese clothing in this period were strongly influenced by the Tang garments, and "professional decorative patterns" adopted and modified from Chinese patterns, including the crane, the ocean waves, the turtle shell, the phoenix and the Kirin, were used specifically for the rank of government officials during the Heian Period. When Japan sent Kenntoushi to China, they also brought their own silver, silk, cotton and fabrics to trade with the Chinese, thus promoting the exchange of garment culture between the two countries.

Now that we have mentioned the Silk Road, we should not ignore the Silk Road over the sea. The so-called

It is said that Guangdong Embroidery has a history of more than 1000 years and was more prevalent after the Ming and Qing Dynasty. Within the country, the Palace Museum has the largest and most representative collections. Guangdong Embroidery's composition is complicated but not disorderly, and its colors are rich and shining. The embroidering pattern is smooth with clear texture and full of changes. Strong and rich primary colors and changes of light and shadow are adopted to make the works a touch of Western paintings. The picture shows a female worker in Chaozhou Embroidery Factory is embroidering a "dragon". (Photo by Huang Yanhong, provided by image library of Hong Kong Traveling in China)

Silk Road over the sea refers to the trade between China and the coastal and island cities of Southeast Asia and Africa over sea route. It appeared in the Eastern Han Dynasty, and came into full bloom in the Yuan and Ming Dynasties. The Roman Empire at that time offered ivory, rhinoceros horns and hawksbill turtle shell to the Eastern Han court, Other countries including Persia (now Iran), India, Sri Lanka and Cambodia brought their pearls, feathers, rhinoceros horns, ivory, spices, hawksbill turtle shells, glass, and cotton into China, while accepting various kinds of Chinese silk fabrics. Through the Tang and Song Dynasties, the Silk Road over the sea reached its peak in the Yuan and Ming Dynasties. The golden brocade and silk fabrics made in Naning, Hangzhou and Suzhou , as well as all kinds of gauze, satin and brocade were sold to Korea, Japan, the Philippines, India, Iran, Iraq, Yemen, Saudi Arabia, Egypt, Morocco, Somalia, and Tanzania. From the second half of the 16th century, the Spaniards occupied the Philippines, and started massive buying of silk from China. A number of sea routes from Manila to various ports in the United States were opened to transport silk from China to America.

The Silk Road across the continent of Eurasia, the Silk Road over the sea, and the Silk Road that connected Southwestern China with the surrounding countries brought the soft and lustrous silk of China to countries in Central Asia, West Asia, South Asia and Europe, along with the technology of silkworm raising, reeling, silk reeling, and weaving of brocade. This was a historical event that gave Chinese garment its great impact on the rest of the world. At the meantime, garments, crafts and styles of other countries had their own profound influence on Chinese garments.

The large-scale economic activities and population flow

(**top**) *Beautiful Chinese silk* (Provided by Imaginechina)
(**middle**) *"Qian Xiang Yi" silk store, located in busy city proper in Qianmen in Beijing, is an old brand store founded in 19th century with high quality goods.* (Provided by Imaginechina)
(**bottom**) *Works of fashion designers shown in a fashion show with the theme of silk.* (Provided by Imaginechina)

Suzhou, located south of the Yangtze River abounds in silk. Suzhou women traditionally are good at embroidery. Excellent geographical environment, splendid and rich brocade and satin, colorful embroidery threads and complicated techniques accumulated from generations make Suzhou embroidery the representative of Chinese embroidery culture. The Chinese traditional pattern peony is elegant and graceful, displaying a unique beauty in exquisite embroidery works. (Provided by Imaginechina)

between China and Central/West Asia made their marks of cultural hybrid in the decorative patterns and styles of garments. In the Han Dynasty textile found in Noyinwula of Inner Mongolia, the winged animals are obviously influenced by the winged animal images of West Asia. In the batik textile unearthed in the Eastern Han Dynasty tomb in Xinjiang, there are typical images of the Gandhara Buddha with deep-set eyes and high-bridged nose, coexisting with dragon patterns typical of central China. The remaining mid section part shows the hind legs and tail of the lion, an animal that came to be known to the Chinese through

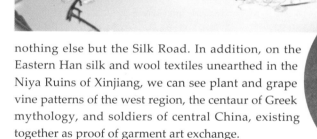

nothing else but the Silk Road. In addition, on the Eastern Han silk and wool textiles unearthed in the Niya Ruins of Xinjiang, we can see plant and grape vine patterns of the west region, the centaur of Greek mythology, and soldiers of central China, existing together as proof of garment art exchange.

The honeysuckle pattern that first became popular in ancient Greece and Rome became popular in Chinese craft along with the entry of Buddhism into China. The symmetrical, balanced and flexible twigs are formed into rippled, circular, square, heart or turtle shell shapes, become intertwining vines for doves and peacocks to rest, or turn into free-style patterns together with the lotus. In some cases, animals and shapes are adapted from Persian art but used to form an auspicious word, a common decorative style in decorative art of China.

Cultural exchange as shown in garment style was most prominent in the most prosperous period of the Tang Dynasty. Merchants from Western Asia and Eastern Europe and from ethnic minority areas of northwestern China brought with them song and dance, musical instruments,

(**top**) *Sichuan embroidery, born in Chengdu, Sichuan Province, is one of the famous traditional Chinese embroidery types. As early as the Han Dynasty, Chengdu's brocade industry was very developed. With soft satin and colored silk as major materials, people embroidered quilt covers, pillow covers, clothes, trousers and painted screens using unique embroidering technique. The picture shows a Chengdu embroidering worker embroidering flowers.* (Photo by Chen Yinian, provided by image library of Hong Kong *Traveling in China*)
(**bottom**) *The embroidery pattern used in the side faces of pillow cover.* (Photo by Lu Zhongmin)

acrobat and the novel lifestyle into Central China through the Silk Road. In the legends about the Xuanzong Emperor, reigning (712-755) of Tang Dynasty and his royal concubine Lady Yang (719-756), a dance of feather cloak in rainbow colors is often mentioned. The feather cloak of the dancer is an integration of ancient India style and traditional Chinese dancewear. Other foreign dances came into central China in the same period, bringing with them dancewear or daily wear of those areas, especially from the western regions.

In the Sui and Tang Dynasties, women came to accept the veil – a large piece of cloth that covers from head to toe. The veil was originally from the northwestern ethnic minority people, used to shield against the dust. When it came to the central regions, the veil became a novel fashion. In the early Tang Dynasty, women had a net-like screen hanging from the brim of the hat, and wore the traditional jacket, skirt and brocade shoes. About a hundred years later, women adopted an entire set of the *hufu* or "alien" costumes from India, Persia and other countries, wearing pointed hat with embroidery, and a close-fitting robe with a turnover collar and tight cuffs, a round collar silk blouse inside, a pair of trousers with narrow leg bottoms and a leather belt, and a pair of high leather boots. The hat, the turnover collar and the leather belt are all distinctive ethnic cloths. By the middle of the Tang Dynasty, the piled-up hair buns and coils and the terracotta rouge were very popular among women. The hairstyle came from western Asia, while the terracotta rough came from Tibet.

The birth and gradual improvement of silk making led to the birth of embroidery, which, as a regional handcraft, adopted distinct regional and ethnic character. In the Spring and Autumn Period, the art of embroidery was already quite mature, as proven in a large quantity of historical relics unearthed in the past hundred years or so. Themes of

Xilankapu means "Tujia flower patterned cloth", which is a kind of local handmade brocade among people of Tujia minority. Tujia girls start to learn weaving technique from their mothers when they are young and must have personally hand-woven Xilankapu as their dowries when they get married, so the craftsmanship can be followed and developed. This is the Tujia's " 万 " patterned brocade. (Photo by Chen Yinian, provided by image library of Hong Kong *Traveling in China*)

Miao Embroidery is a kind of unique Chinese embroidery art. Patterns of flowers and birds are embroidered on materials of garments and home decorations, displaying a sense of primitive simplicity. (Photo by Wang Miao, provided by image library of Hong Kong *Traveling in China*)

embroidery in this period include exaggerated figures of dragon, phoenix and tiger, interspersed with flowers, foliage or geometrical shapes. There is often a great sense of rhythm brought out by the vivid animal figures, the decorative patterns, and the richness and harmony of colors.

Entering the Qin and Han Dynasties, embroidery reached a new height. What deserves special mention is the workshop set up in Linzi, capital of the Qi Kingdom, dedicated exclusively to the making of official court uniforms. Thousands of weavers were hired, and no cost was spared. Not only the royal family had the whole house dress in brocade and their horses and dogs clad in woolen dress, but all the rich wore what was called the "five colored brocade" and decorated their furniture with silks and embroideries. By the end of the late Han Dynasty, Buddhism became increasingly popular in China. Embroidery of Buddha's portrait remained popular all the way through the Tang Dynasty. This kind of embroidered Buddha can still be seen in museums in England and in Japan, acclaimed for the fine craftsmanship and dazzling colors. Another great achievement of the Tang embroidery art is the invention of a new stitch – the satin stitch, which is popular until the present day. This new stitch brought more freedom to the artist, and brought about a new era of embroidery.

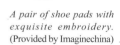

A pair of shoe pads with exquisite embroidery. (Provided by Imaginechina)

The Song Dynasty marks the peak of Chinese embroidery, both in terms of quality and quantity. The refinement of embroidery in the Tang and Song Dynasties was determined by the social environment of that time. In a time of clear division of labor between men and women with men ploughing and women weaving, all women were required to learn needlecraft. Embroidery was a basic skill, a prerequisite for a woman to be accepted by society, and at the same time an elegant pastime, hobby from which women of leisure cultivated their artistic taste and creativity. The function of embroidery can be classified into daily necessities and art pieces intended strictly for artistic appreciation. Even the intelligentsia participated in the creative process of fine embroidery, which often borrowed ideas from painters before it was completed by artisans.

The revival of folk handicraft in the Ming Dynasty injected new vitality into the technique and production of embroidery. Individuals and households talented in embroidery became famous for their crafts, and both the demand and usage of embroidery increased. Practical embroidery pieces became better in quality, finer in material, and more skilled in techniques. In the Ming and later Qing Dynasties, embroidery reached its peak in popularity. In the two hundred plus years of the Qing Dynasty, local schools of embroidery appeared like bamboo shoots after the rain, the most famous being Suzhou, Guangdong, Sichuan, Hunan, Beijing and Shandong schools. In addition to their local flavors, these schools all borrowed from other ethnic cultures.

Today, fashion comes and goes, and machines have replaced the human hand in many ways. Fortunately, the art and craft of embroidery have been preserved as China's great cultural heritage. Besides the local embroidery schools, many ethnic minority people have their own beautiful embroidery, such as the Uygur, the Yi, the Dai, the Bouyi, the Kazak, the Yao, the Miao, the Tujia, the Jingpo, the Dong, the Bai, the Zhuang, the Mongolian, and the Tibetan people. Embroidery is not only found in garments and home furnishings, but also exists on their own as a unique art form that has incorporated the character of Chinese painting and calligraphy.

"Peony and phoenix facing the sun" is a classical pattern for Chinese silk, showing a sense of luckiness and happiness. This is a work of wood block New Year picture made in Taohuawu of Suzhou, Jiangsu Province. (Collected by Wang Shucun)

Beizi: a Song Style Garment

The most commonly found garment of the Song Dynasty is the *beizi* , a front closure overcoat that is not fastened in front so that the inner coat is shown. The *beizi* can be in different lengths – above the knee, below the knee, or ankle length. The sleeves can be either broad or narrow. There can be either side slits reaching as high as the armpits, or none at all.

It is quite a curious phenomenon that the *beizi* is popular among people of both sexes and all social strata at the same time. In Song paintings, we can find both aristocratic women and maidservants' wearing *beizi* of basically the same style.

The *beizi* was preferred by men of the Song Dynasty as an informal wear at home because of its unfastened front, the relaxed waistline and its flexibility in length

An image of Song lady wearing a front closure overcoat with a straight collar and tight sleeves. (Painted by Gao Chunming, selected from *Lady Garments and Adornments of Chinese Past Dynasties* written by Zhou Xun and Gao Chunming)

52

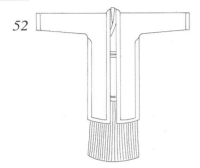

The sketch drawing for the front piece of beizi. *(Painted by Hua Mei)*

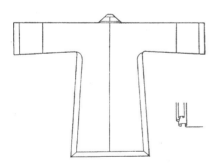

The sketch drawing of the back of a beizi. *(Painted by Zang Yingchun)*

Part of Listening to Qin *painted by Song Hui Emperor (1082-1135). The person who plays in the painting is the author of this painting. The emperor also wore a long robe called beizi in his spare time, which showed the popularity of the dress.*

and width. In a painting called *Tuning the Zither*, which was said to have been done by the Zhao Ji, the Hui Emperor of the Song Dynasty, the emperor himself was seen wearing the *beizi* in a dark colored material. In Song Dynasty paintings in the Dunhuang Grottos, a famous character was found wearing the *beizi*, whereas the same character in the Tang Dynasty painting was still wearing a round collared gown commonly found in Tang costumes.

Although there seems to be no social status or sex attached to the *beizi*, it is still more common to find it on people of the higher or middle strata. The heavy

laborers preferred short jackets and trousers for their convenience. What people of higher or middle social strata wear, it seems, are more reflective of the cultural and aesthetic aspirations of that time, and Song Dynasty is no exception. The popularity of *beizi* in the Song Dynasty is closely related in the cultural development of that era. The silhouette of the Song *beizi* is straight, as compared to the curvaceous shape of the Tang garments with open collar, wide skirt and the fluid veil covering the entire body. In general, Tang people were much more extravagant in the way they dressed, while the Song people preferred the reserved and contained elegance. The psychological orientation of the Song garment seemed to be more in line with the prevalent ideology of the time – a sense of order that was to be obeyed between the emperor and his subordinates, the father and the son, the husband and the wife. Any desire of the individual had to take the back seat.

The classic Chinese aesthetics was played to the fullest in the Song Dynasty, as reflected in the white walls and black tiles in architecture, the single colored glaze in ceramics, and the casual and free style of landscape painting in art. Even plants and flowers were given different human characters, so that the plum blossom, the orchid, the bamboo

A Song Dynasty porcelain bottle with twisting clouds pattern made in Jizhou kiln.

The excavated material object of a man's beizi. *(Photo by Jin Baoyuan)*

and the chrysanthemum were appreciated not only for their external appearance but also for the virtues with which they were endowed. Compared to anything that tried to win the admiration and curiosity of others, the Song people preferred the simple elegance of the *beizi*, which reflects the "less is more" sense of beauty of people at that time.

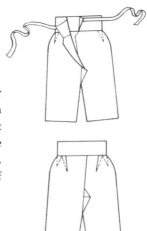

The structural sketch drawings for Song Dynasty lady trousers. (Front & Back) (Painted according to excavated relics in Huangsheng Tomb in Fuzhou, selected from *Research on Ancient Chinese Clothes and Adornments* written by Shen Congwen)

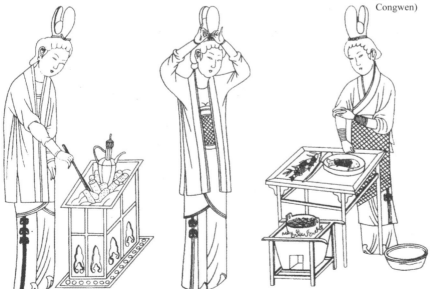

The daily dress image of women of the Song Dynasty. (Selected from *Research on Ancient Chinese Clothes and Adornments* written by Shen Congwen)

Ming Garments as Seen in Classical Portraits

Portraits were once popular in the Ming Dynasty. Thanks to the realistic, portrayal and vivid rendering of the artists, we now have a good understanding of the garment and ornament details. Influenced by the portrait art, other painting styles followed the same realism when reflecting the lives of people at that time.

Ming was the last dynasty in which men wore the skirt. In a famous painting by the Song painter called the *Peaceful Pleasures*, farmers were still wearing the short skirt, regardless of whether they were sitting on the buffalo back or walking in the fields. This type of pleated, knee-length skirt can still be found in some clown figures in Beijing opera. Below the skirt the shorts or long pants are revealed.

Images most frequently found in portraits were those of government officials and scholars, who wore scholar caps or casual

A human image of the Ming Dynasty shown in a painting. (Provided by Hua Mei)

square caps, long robes, and sometimes holding a horsetail "Buddha duster." In a Ming tomb found in west of Yangzhou, a full set of scholar's dress was unearthed, among which was a scholar's cap with hanging ends, a gown with dark rimmed round collar and broad sleeves and high boots made with felt. Similar garment style survived through Beijing Opera costumes, so that we can easily tell a Chinese scholar when we see one.

57

A lady bellyband of the Ming Dynasty. (Painted by Gao Chunming, selected from *Lady Garments and Adornments of Chinese Past Dynasties* written by Zhou Xun and Gao Chunming)

Women's costume of the Ming Dynasty went even further in its gentle and elegant beauty, which is often recognized as the epitome of classic Chinese female garment. The Ming Dynasty is a period in which the Chinese Han culture developed to the fullest, absorbing the cultural essence of the previous Tang and Song Dynasties. Ever since the Ming Dynasty and up until the present day, visual representation of ancient Chinese females or women in mythologies has mostly adopted the Ming style. The Ming women wore robes of rough homespun cloths without gold embroidery, and the colors were limited to purple, green and fuchsia. Red, deep blue and bright red were strictly forbidden for women commoners to wear, so as not to confuse with the royal garment colors.

The most typical Ming women's garment is the *bijia*, a long sleeveless jacket that drapes all the way down to below the knee or even lower. Embroidery is superimposed on woven textures, and at the front closure, a jade ornament is often attached. We can easily find women clad in this type of sleeveless jacket in Ming paintings. A slender figure was the ideal of beauty for Ming women. The *bijia* helped create a visual impression of slenderness.

In comparison with the Tang *ruqun*, the Ming women's garments were less lavish but more gentle and elegant. Neither was it as stiff and rigid as the Song women's wear. A closer look at how they dress can tell us that these women were not as flippant as the Tang women were. They seemed much more reserved and subdued in their proper-fitting long gowns with woven patterns. Often the gowns are tied with a bow at the waist, the end draping all the way down below the knees. Ornaments included silk ribbons at the waist tied in decorative knots, jade ornaments between the knots, and hairpins for grownup women. The entire set of garments is

The New Year Picture The Snow on the Shanhai Pass *made in Yangliuqing, Tianjin shows the image of Ming Dynasty men wearing skirts.* (Collected by Wang Shucun)

carefully put together for an overall effect of elegance, but not extravagance.

The Ming *ruqun* was more similar to the Song Dynasty *ruqun* in overall appearance. The most obvious change in the Ming Dynasty was the addition of a short waist skirt on young maidservants, intended, possibly, to serve as an apron that protects the longer robe underneath. This waist skirt becomes an added layer, as we can see in Ming paintings, which flow with movement with its natural soft pleats. In artistic representations, this makes up the image of a lively girl, together with coiled hair buns.

The development of theatre and novels in the Yuan and Ming Dynasties bought about the flourishing of the woodblock carving illustrations. Hundreds of illustrations are found in literary work that help us understand the dress style of the scholar, the lady, the maidservant, the old lady, the dancer, the village girl, the carter, the fisherman, the boatman, the servant, the monk, the child. We also get to see the beggar, the porter, the court runner, the farmer, the merchant, as well as the outlaws and the buffalo boy. Although the story is not always of Ming Dynasty, the artwork done by Ming artisans cannot help but reflecting more of the Ming characteristics.

The Official Uniform

Clothing and ornaments can often reveal one's social status, and this is particularly true in the rigidly stratified feudal society. In ancient China, how one dressed was not merely a matter of folk customs, but was an integral part of the State rules on ceremony and propriety. In each dynasty there were clearly defined rules and decrees on the material, color, decorative pattern and style of dress, distinguishing the royal, the civil and military officials and the commoners. Anyone dressing against this code was severely punished. This practice of regulating and defining the ranks of officials and the commoners was apparently intended at upholding the order of the ruling class, but contributed to the diversity of Chinese garments.

The mention of ancient Chinese official uniforms

The image of an ancient official wearing a black gauze cap shown in New Year pictures. (Colleted by Wang Shucun)

A portrait of Minamotono Yoritomo, which shows the dress image of the upper classes of Japan can be traced to the same origin with China. Yoritomo was the founder of Kamakura Bakufu, who almost reigned Japan at the beginning of 13th century.

almost always leads to the Chinese opera type of character – one dressed in a round collar gown, a black gauze cap with wings on each side, a white jade belt and black boots with white sole. In reality, Chinese official uniform is by far more complex than that. Each dynasty had rules of its own, which could be changed many times even within a dynasty.

There is no official uniform without the cap. In Han Dynasty, civil officials wore caps with a *ze* or kerchief lining the cap, while the military officials wore a hat designed for their ranks. Men of all social strata in Qin and Han Dynasties all wore a kerchief, the only difference being that the commoners wore no cap or hat above it. In Wei, Jin, and Southern and Northern Dynasties, officials wore gauze hats, which were painted and stiffened with lacquer.

Both officials and the common people in the Tang Dynasty wore *futou* or turbans. The early *futou* was just a close-fitting piece of cloth wrapped around the head. Later on a kerchief was put under the turban padded with wood, silk, grass or leather to form the shape of hair buns. After the mid Tang Dynasty, the cap finally took shape, still given the name *futou*. The two corners of the *futou* are round or wide, tipping slightly upwards.

The Song Dynasty *futou* was unique in that it had two straight tips protruding at both sides, intended, some say, at preventing officials getting their heads too close to whisper when in court.

Later on the official headdress evolved from the *futou* of Tang and Song Dynasties to the black gauze cap of the Ming Dynasty. There were no significant changes to the style. The difference was that the turban, which could be wrapped and unwrapped, became a cap of a fixed shape. "Black gauze cap" also became a synonym for the government official status, used until the present day. No significant changes were made in the Tang, Song and Ming official gowns. There were clear rules specifying the appropriate color for each of the ranks, with slight modifications made in each dynasty. This system was passed down until the Qing Dynasty ended in history.

In Tang Dynasty the woman emperor Wuzetian had all official

The head wrapping scarf was usually made of black etamine. The style evolved from soft and slanting forward to hard with a square shape, but the major styles were about 3-5 types. (Selected from Research on Ancient Chinese Clothes and Adornments *written by Shen Congwen)*

The clothes for Tang Dynasty civil officials. The styles of robes, hats and shoes were slightly different. (Selected from Research on Ancient Chinese Clothes and Adornments *written by Shen Congwen)*

62

The handed down Ming Dynasty ornamental patches Buzi *showing official rank for civil officials. (Painted by Hua Mei)*
The first rank: the celestial crane
The second rank: the golden pheasant
The third rank: the peacock
The fourth rank: the wild goose
The fifth rank: the silver pheasant
The sixth rank: the egret
The seventh rank: the purple mandarin duck
The eighth rank: the yellow bird
The ninth rank: the quail
Officials doing odd jobs: the magpie

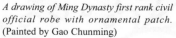

A drawing of Ming Dynasty first rank civil official robe with ornamental patch.
(Painted by Gao Chunming)

The handed down Ming Dynasty ornamental patches showing official rank for military officials. (From left to right and from the top down, painted by Hua Mei)
The first rank: the lion
The second rank: the lion
The third rank: the tiger
The fourth rank: the leopard
The fifth rank: the brown bear
The sixth rank: the younger tiger
The seventh rank: the younger tiger
The eighth rank: the rhinoceros
The ninth rank: the sea horse

Several typical ancient official hats and dresses. (Selected from *Research on Ancient Chinese Clothes and Adornments* written by Shen Congwen)

wear embroidered gowns, specifying that civil official gowns were embroidered with birds and military official gowns with beasts. The Ming dynasty followed this tradition, distinguishing types and ranks of officials with *buzi*, embroidered pieces attached to the chest and back of gowns indicating the wearers' ranks.

To the ruling class of early Qing Dynasty who was intent on defining rigid court ceremonies, the official attire was used as an important instrument to distinguish social status. The Qing rulers invented the most complicated system of official attire in Chinese history, strictly defining the color, decorative patterns and style of official uniform in books with clear illustrations, intended to be passed down to all generations to come. The court even set up supervisory office ensuring that all rules are followed in the making of official uniform, and all court attire are complete with the most refined weaving and embroidery, and complimented with complete set of ornaments.

The most distinguishing elements of the Qing official uniform are the horse-hoof shaped sleeve and the Mandarin jacket style. However, the use of *buzi*, or ornament patches, was borrowed directly from the previous Ming Dynasty. The court insignia badges clearly distinguished the civil and military officials with embroideries of birds or beasts. Emblems with different animals were used to further distinguish the ranks and authority of these officials. The emblems embroidered on the decorative patches were however different from the Ming Dynasty in that they were much more decorative, often accentuated with an elaborately embroidered border. In terms of style, the Qing *buzi* was embroidered on the outer jacket worn over the gown with front closure, and the front embroidery was done in two pieces at each side. The black gauze cap of the Ming Dynasty was replaced by the Hualing or feathered cap. The number of "eyes" on the peacock feather was used to differentiate each different rank. The official court uniform and daily uniform were both worn in different layers of robe, jacket, gown, vest, and decorative patches, complimented by court beads, court belt, jade ornaments, colored silk ribbons and perfumed sachel. Officials wore court beads made of jade, agate, coral, or sandalwood, and silk ribbons of bright yellow, turquoise or azurite, all according to their ranks.

Female relatives of the officials also wore elaborately decorated dresses. Inlaid brims were lavishly used in their dresses, complimented by pearls, jade ornaments and embroideries on the hemline, the chest and the sleeve edges. Pleats were fixed with silk threads, and even the sole of socks and shoes invisible to others were covered with embroideries. This attitude was passed down by the most privileged

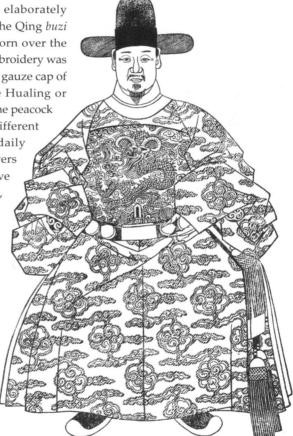

Wearing a gauze hat, jade belt and hanging a drooping board and a plate with tassels and decorating chest part with ornamental patch similar to python pattern. This is a marquis official robe of Ming Dynasty. (Selected from *History of Chinese Ancient Garments* written by Zhou Xibao)

This New Year picture shows the dress image of Qing officials of all different ranks. (Colleted by Wang Shucun)

throughout the dynasties, in which only the most leisurely could have appreciated the intricacy of these details.

Out of all details in Chinese official uniform, the *buzi* was the most outstanding feature to mark the relationship of garment and power. These ornament patches had birds and beasts of all kinds, both real and mythical. For civil officials, real birds such as cranes, golden pheasants, peacocks, wild geese, silver pheasants, egrets, larks and quails were used, together with mythical birds that look like a cross between an egret and a peacock. In the *buzi* of military officials, there were recognizable animals such as tigers, lions and panthers, as well as beasts apparently coming out of someone's imagination. Different animals were used to signify different ranks.

Ancient Armor Suits

No elaborate and vivid description of the military uniforms could be found in ancient Chinese books. In ancient Chinese mythology, Chi You, the "god of war" (from 5000 years ago), invented the armor. That period of transition from tribal allegiance to the state was a period of volatility and frequent wars. The emergence of the armor was inseparable from the appearance of wars. To guard against the attack of stone arrows and wooden axes, people of the tribal period very likely used protective instruments made from canes, wood or leather.

The early armor suits only covered the head and the chest, whereas later they developed into separate pieces of the body shield, the shoulder shields and the leg shields. Judging from artifacts excavated in early times, the bronze helmet appeared in as early as the Shang Dynasty. In Zhou Dynasty, bronze helmet and

The ichnography for the Song Dynasty armor. (Painted by Li Ling according to *Portraits of Officials with Outstanding Service Stored in Lingyan Pavilion*)

The ichnography for the Qin Dynasty armor. (Painted by Zhou Xun)

chest shield made of rhinoceros or buffalo hide were used in wars. It was also recorded in early history that at that time officials in charge of armored suits, which were made with round pieces in groups of seven, painted in white, red and black. An elaborately embroidered robe was worn over the armored suit to display the dignity of the army, removed only when the actual fighting began.

The Warring States Period was one with incessant wars among the warlords. In that period, however, significant scientific and cultural development took place, together with the rapid progress in military related manufacturing. Official document of that time recorded the complicated process and craft of making leather armored suites, detailing the form, measurements, structure and proportions of each part of the shield. It was clear that each state attached great importance to the making of the armored suits. Metal shields, according to historical artifacts,

The tomb figures of foot soldiers excavated from Emperor Qin Shi Huang's terracotta warriors archeological site. (Selected from *Research on Ancient Chinese Clothes and Adornments* written by Shen Congwen)

appeared in the mid of the Warring States Period, as a simple chest shield shaped like an animal face. The shield was made with metal plates linked together, and at about the same time iron helmet made its entry into the scene. In a later excavation, a helmet made from 89 iron pieces was found in a tomb burial in the Yan state.

Judging from the terracotta warrior burials and the accompanying stone burial armors, it is apparent that armor suits made of iron were already prevalent in the Qin Dynasty, although leather was also used very often. The Qin Dynasty, it seems, was a transition period for armor suit materials. The move away from leathered armor suits towards iron was primarily due to the replacement of bronze weapons by much sharper iron weapons in the period between the Warring States Period and the Han Dynasty. In short, sharper weapons

Han Dynasty cavalrymen (Selected from *Research on Ancient Chinese Clothes and Adornments* written by Shen Congwen)

called for greater protection devices.

The excavation of a large number of terracotta warriors in the Emperor Qin Shihuang Tomb has provided us a complete set of visual images of the Chinese armor suits of that time. The unearthed soldier figures included foot soldiers, army clerks, riders and archers, all with armors that strictly reflect their rank and status. Generals and riders wore hats, while ordinary soldiers did not. Although they were not real artifacts of armor suits, the fine artisanship put into these clay figures were so meticulous that the structure of the armor was clearly seen. The most common armor style, the style for common soldiers, had one distinct feature – all metal chips were covered like fish scale by the piece on top of them at the chest, and in the reverse direction at waist level, a design intended for easy movement. Looking from the central line, all chips cover the next outwards. Construction of shoulder chips was similar to the waist. Chips at the shoulders, waist and below the neck were connected with belts and nails, from two nails to four and no more than six. The length of the armor is equal at front and back, rounded at the lower edges with no additional decoration. Materials we have today on Qin armor indicate that armor of the same type is similar in style, measurement, construction and number of chips. This can be seen as the result of measurement unification

Hang Dynasty armors for generals. (Painted by Zou Zhenya, selected from *Lady Garments and Adornments of Chinese Past Dynasties* written by Zhou Xun and Gao Chunming)

71

promoted by Emperor Qin Shihuang, and shows that the production of armor was centralized instead of privately done.

The gradual maturity and perfection of the Qin armor was no coincidence. On one hand, the fine quality was a direct result of frequent wars among states. On the other hand, the development of armor itself had gone through over two thousand years of history from the late primitive period to the Qin Dynasty. The craft of leather armor was already quite advanced, reaching its height in the Qin Dynasty. By the Han Dynasty, it began to be replaced by the new armor made of iron.

In the Western Han Period, iron armor became the prevalent armor, and a necessity for the army fittings. Soldiers and generals alike wore the *chanyi* (a kind of under shirt) and trousers. The *chanyi* is very similar to the *shenyi* in style. Army wear of the Han Dynasty were red or crimson.

Incessant wars through the ages led to even greater development in armor suits in the Wei, Jin, Southern and Northern Dynasties. Weapons became sharper, armors and helmets stronger. Typical armor suit of this period included the barrel sleeve suit, the double layer suit and the Mingguang suit. The barrel sleeve suit is normally made of fish-scale or tortoise-shell like chips that are joined together. Protective barrel sleeves are attached at the shoulders. A helmet is worn with ear protectors and decorative tassels. The double-layered suit is closer in style to the daily wear. It is mostly made with metal although those made with animal skin have also been found. The suit is in two pieces on front and back, covering the chest and the back respectively, similar to a vest that runs down to below the belly.

The ichnography for the Song Dynasty armor. (Painted by Zou Zhenya)

Mingguang suit is one with round metal plates protecting the chest and the back, worn with a leather belt and wide trousers. This type of armor became more popular over the ages and gradually replaced the double layer suit. In historical books, it was clearly said that both soldiers and their horses wore protective armors.

The most commonly used armor in the Sui Dynasty was the double-layered suit and the Mingguang suit. The double-layered suit improved with smaller fish-scale chips, and extended to the belly so that leather armor skirt was no longer necessary. The bottom of the suit was made of crescent or lotus-leave shaped chips for better protection below the waist. The form of the Mingguang armor was similar to the previous dynasties, only with longer trouser legs.

A series of reforms were done on garment styles, including reforms of army suits. There were thirteen

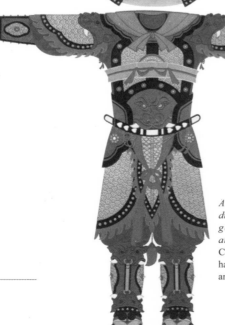

A three-dimensional drawing of Ming Dynasty generals' helmet and armor. (Painted by Gao Chunming according to handed down stone carving and paintings)

The ichnography for a waistcoat armor. (Painted by Hua Mei)

types of armor suit designated as official army wear, made with materials from copper to wood, leather and cloth. Iron and leather suits were used in actual wars, whereas decorative armor suits made with silk and cotton, visually pleasing as they were, were used as daily wear or ceremonial suit for generals. More decorations were found in the Tang helmet, suit and boots. There were more decorations, carvings and metal plates. The chips were better formed for ease of movement. At the prime of the Tang Dynasty, the strong national power led to a more peaceful time. The once practical armor suits became more decorative than functional. The suits were painted, and even the inner garments were embroidered with animals.

In ancient China, greater protection in the armor suit was often achieved by increasing the number of chips. Chips became heavier and heavier through the ages. There were two kinds of armor suits in the Song

"Ruan Kao" is a suit of light armor used in Chinese operas. The military official shown in this New Year picture wears a scale-armor and a feather commander-in-chief helmet and inserts four flags. (Produced in Yangliuqing, Tianjin, collected by Wang Shucun)

Dynasty, one for use in actual fight and the other for ceremonial purposes. According to *Song History*, the entire suit had 1825 pieces of chips that were connected with leather threads. The total weight was approximately 25 kilograms. Paper suit existed as well, with chips made of folded soft paper joined with nail fasteners. Delicate as they seemed, they were hard to penetrate with arrows. As for ceremonial armor suits, the face was made with yellow silk while the lining was made with cotton cloth. Chips were painted on with a yellowish green color, complete with edging decoration of red brocade, black trousers, red leather ribbons and painted faces on front and back. The paper armor suit

(Italy) Part of Lang Shining's Deer Hunting, *which shows garments worn for riding and hunting when Manchu noble men hunting in hunting ground. Deer hunting was a kind of imperial hunting activity with the function of both entertainment and practicing military skills. The drawing was painted in 1741.*

was an invention of the Song Dynasty. However, we can no longer find out how these were made. There were guesses that the suit was made of silkworm paper, light, durable and strong. History books of that time had recorded the exchange for a paper suit with several sets of fine metal suits, thus validating our estimate of its high quality and value.

By the Ming Dynasty, cotton armor was widely used in the army, which was light and better suited to a war of firearms. When making the cotton suit, cotton was hammered repeatedly and then fastened with nail fasteners.

Qing Dynasty, however, was a period with the most significant changes in the development of ancient martial attire. The Manchu, as the ruling people, made their own reforms of the Han military wear. The use of guns and cannons lead further to this transformation. The Qing Dynasty armor suits were divided into coat of mail and *weishang*. On each shoulder of the coat of mail, there is a protective shoulder pad, under which there is an armpit guard. In addition, metal chest plates

The New Year picture Female Students Practicing Military Drill *produced in Wuqiang, Hebei Province, shows the scenes of female students from the new concepts schools with short coats and belts carrying guns on their shoulders at the end of the Qing Dynasty.* (Collected by Wang Shucun)

"Boy scout on short horses" is a famous folk activity held among people of Debaozhuang ethnic group in Guangxi. Helmets worn by kids have an ancient flavor. (Photo by Chen Yinian)

were attached on front and back, and a trapezoid shaped belly protector was added as well. The left side of the body is protected, while the right remains open for carrying bow and arrows. The double width *weishang* was used to protect the sides, fastened around the waist when needed. Helmets, whether made of iron or cattle hide, were painted on the surface. On all four sides of the helmet, there were vertical ridges, a brow protector and metal tubing for attaching the decorative feather, tassel or animal fur. A protective silk collar is attached for shielding the neck and the ears, decorated with fine embroidery and metal tacks. By the end of the Qing Dynasty, army uniform for the navy, the infantry and the police patrol already had distinct Western features.

Tang Dynasty soldiers wearing armors. (Painted according to Tang Dynasty frescoes in Dunhuang, selected from *Research on Ancient Chinese Clothes and Adornments* written by Shen Congwen)

Qi Costumes – a Combination of Manchu and Han Nationality's Clothes

At the mention of the Qing Dynasty (1616-1911) costumes, the first image that comes into people's mind is men's long robes and mandarin jackets as well as women's gowns – with loose-bodied waistline in early time and then gradually tight waistline matched with a waistcoat outside becoming more popular. In fact, these impressions are not sufficient enough to represent the costume image of the Qing Dynasty, which spans nearly three hundred years in Chinese history.

Manchu people's life environment, production mode and life style had changed dramatically since they crossed the Great Wall from Northeast, settled in the middle land of China, took control of the national power and founded the Qing Dynasty. Manchu

Manchu women wore robes instead of skirts, and robes were their common daily dresses. (Painted by Zhou Xun, selected from *Lady Garments and Adornments of Chinese Past Dynasties* written by Zhou Xun and Gao Chunming)

traditional costumes, which are designed to facilitate riding and shooting, are very different from the Han nationality's costumes. In order to exterminate the Han people's national consciousness, the rulers of the Qing Dynasty forbid the Han people to wear Han costumes with strict order and forced them to take off their *dajin* (a style of clothes which button to the left and with overlapping front garment pieces) coats and robes, skirts and trousers and put on Manchu collarless *duijin* (a style of clothes with buttons in the middle) coats, gowns and long trousers. One thing that irritated the Han people the most was the order to shave the forehead and leave a big pigtail at the back of the head

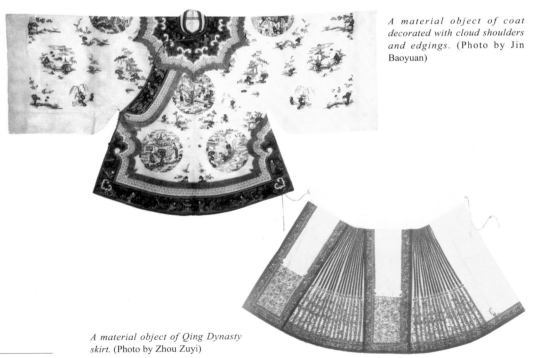

A material object of coat decorated with cloud shoulders and edgings. (Photo by Jin Baoyuan)

A material object of Qing Dynasty skirt. (Photo by Zhou Zuyi)

Imperial women of Qing Dynasty wearing different styles of daily dresses. The two in the left wear cheong-sams and the two in the right wear waistcoats with long pleated skirts. (Selected from Research on Ancient Chinese Clothes and Adornments *written by Shen Congwen)*

according to the Manchu' tradition. Many Han people who insisted on the Ming's customs of wearing square scarf and refused to shave their hair were killed. And this arose great discontentment among the Hans, so rebellions took place in some places. Some Han people would rather to have a shaven head as a monk. Some people painted a Ming's square scarf on their head to show their faithfulness to their homeland's traditional costumes. Some used words to show their inner hatred indirectly by naming themselves as *shoufa*, which means to keep their hair. This situation of severe rivalry forced the Qing government to adopt some relevant transient policies to ease up the governing crisis caused by the hair shaving and costumes change. Costumes of men, government officials, adults, Confucian scholars, prostitutes must follow the Manchu tradition; while women, *yanmen* runners, youngsters, children, monks, Taoists, and the costumes used in theater, funeral, wedding might follow the Han tradition. As a result, from the beginning to the

A material object of cheong-sam with colorful embroidery and edgings popular at the end of the Qing Dynasty. (Photo by Zhou Zuyi)

A chart of women's lip-painting styles in past dynasties

(Edited by Gao Chunming, selected from *Lady Garments and Adornments of Chinese Past Dynasties* written by Zhou Xun and Gao Chunming)

midterm years of the Qing Dynasty, Manchu women differed greatly from the Han women in hairstyles, clothes and shoes.

Manchu women didn't wear skirts but robes with trousers inside, which were their most common daily clothes. The ceremonial robes that Manchu lady wore were decorated with "horse hoof sleeves," complicated ornaments and accessories. There were two types of daily robes; the long shirt that one would wear separately and the cloak. The long shirt was round-neck, "button to the right side" style and long enough to reach feet with twisted garment pieces, straight clothes body and sleeves, edgings, five buttons and no vents. In terms of the sleeve, there were the ones with sleeves or without sleeves. And the materials used were mainly floss for embroidery, woven pattern fabrics and fabrics with golden thread. The shirt was usually decorated by edgings. The cloak was worn outside the under linens with vents on both sides that reach the oxter and the top of the vent was decorated with cloud pattern. Mostly for formal occasions, cloaks were decorated

The Han Dynasty	
The Wei Dynasty	
The Tang Dynasty	
The Tang Dynasty	
The Tang Dynasty	
The Song Dynasty	
The Ming Dynasty	
The Qing Dynasty	
The Qing Dynasty	

An image of Han lady in the Qing Dynasty wearing a robe, skirt and waistcoat. (A wood block New Year picture produced in Yanliuqing, Tianjin, collected by Wang Shucun)

with complicate and delicate edgings and patterns. As robes usually had no collars, noble ladies liked to wear a little scarf even when they were at home. In early times, robes were very loose-bodied, and then became tighter and tighter. Till the end of the Qing Dynasty, the underarm part of the robe was not very tight and the garment outline was basically flat and straight. Collars, sleeves and the garment pieces were decorated with wide lacework. The length of robe didn't change.

Manchu women combed their hair into a flat chignon at the back with two horns supported by a hair board, which was also called "double horns hair style."Very beautiful and unique, they often decorated hair with big flowers of vivid color or tassels. Manchu women originally didn't have the footbinding tradition. Their shoes are very characteristic. It is a style of shoes with a high heel in the middle of the sole. The wood heel is generally 3cm to 6cm, but some are even as high as 15 cm. The shape of wooden heel is like a flowerpot, so it is called "flower pot sole." If the shape of the heel is like a horse hoof, then it is called "horse hoof sole."

The Han women in the early years of Qing Dynasty still maintained their two-piece dressing features by wearing upper coats and lower skirts separately. They usually wore coats and skirts with trousers inside. Those who wore trousers without the matching skirts outside were generally lowborn. Upper clothes, from inside to outside included belly-covers, undercoats, coats, waistcoats and cloaks etc. The backless belly-cover was hung around neck by a silver chain. Undercoats were usually made by silk, satin or soft cloth with vivid and bright colors such as pink, peach red, cerise or light green. For different seasons, there were unlined, lined, leather and cotton coats. Sleeves were rather tight in early times, and then gradually loosened, but till the end of the Qing, short and small style was once more popular. Waistcoats were mostly worn in cold days in spring and autumn. Cloaks were the clothes worn in cold weather when going outside. Cloaks of noble family were usually embroidered by colorful golden threads and decorated with all kinds of jewelries.

There was a wide variety of types and styles of Han women's skirts, and this was well represented by the development and change in skirt fashion. In early years of the Qing Dynasty, the "moonlight skirt" was once very popular, which was made by ten pieces of cloth that was tucked into tens of pleats. Each pleat was in a different color and painted carefully. The color was light and elegant, like bright moon light. Another type was to use many colors in one pleat, like the moonlight halation. There was another type called the "Chinese ink painting skirt," which used cloth with simple but elegant background color. The cloth was then printed with pattern of scattered flowers. The skirt had the charm of the Chinese ink painting and looked very elegant. During the reign of Kangxi and Qianlong, the

Manchu women in the Qing Dynasty wore waistcoats outside robes and combed "double ends" hairstyle. (Provided by Hua Mei)

"phoenix tail skirt" prevailed. The outside of underskirt was decorated with narrow long ribbons made by all different colors of silk and satin. Each strip of ribbon was embroidered with different patterns, and both edges were decorated with golden threads or laces. The skirt looked very fancy and luxurious. This style of skirt was mostly for women from rich families, but normal family's women would try to buy one for their wedding occasion. Since the middle period of the Qing Dynasty, people had exerted more creativity on the skirt design based on the previous skirt fashion. They tucked the cloth into very thin pleats. From the material object we could see today, there was one skirt with more than

*At the end of 19ᵗʰ century, some open-minded officials sent their daughters to study in Europe and America. And they brought back Euro-American garments and adornments. (*Western Garments* painted by Wu Youru)*

three hundred pleats. The skirt hem was embroidered with water pattern. The water pattern would be partly hidden and partly visible when its wearer started to walk, which made the skirt look very dazzling. Later, pleats were joined with silk threads, so that they could be tightened and loosened flexibly. The skirt looked like fish scale, so it was called the "fish scale pleated skirt." At the end of the Qing, there appeared skirts that were decorated with ribbons. The ribbon was cut into the shape of a sword, and its sharp corner was decorated with gold, silver and bronze bells. The skirt not only looked very fancy and dazzling, but also would make euphonious tinkly sound when its wearer walked around.

In those years, there was a kind of beautiful ornament for lady garments. The ornament was put on shoulder parts, and the four corners in front, back and two shoulders were all made in the shape of cloud. As it was very similar to the Chinese lucky sign - *ruyi*, this type of ornament was called the "cloud shoulder." There were layers of tassels hung from the edges on this ornament. First appeared in the Tang Dynasty, but became popular in the Qing Dynasty, this type of ornaments was an indispensable part of wedding and ceremonial costumes.

In middle and later years of the Qing Dynasty, there was no big difference between Manchu and Han women's daily clothes. Their common features were loose-bodied robes covering outside the standard Chinese slim and weak beautiful ladies with slopping shoulders, wasp waist, and flat chest. No bizarre dresses were allowed at that time.

In early years of the Qing Dynasty, Han women's hairstyle was similar to the Ming Dynasty. They combed flat, low and fitted hair bun. Since middle years, they had started to imitate the Qing royal maid and considered high hair bun as fashionable. Till the end of the Qing Dynasty, round hair bun at the back of the head prevailed. Unmarried women wore long plaits or double horn buns or double whorl buns. Also in this period of time, originally a kind of young girl's hairstyle called "hair bang" – eyebrow- high short hair at forehead, was the rage for women of all ages.

The Han women also liked to decorate their hair bun with flowers, with fresh flowers and kingfisher's feather the most fashionable. In wintertime, especially during the traditional Chinese New Year, women of different ages all liked to wear red or pink color silk flowers. These flowers were usually made into a certain pattern with lucky meaning. Women in the north liked to plug one or two silver hairpins in

小兒怒

小兒說孩兒愛爺娘爺娘不愛
兒心傷孩兒想要強爺娘不愛
叫上學堂爺娘說我愛孩
兒不愛錢有了學堂你
爭兒小兒說皇帝常
把旨意下為何官員
不聽話爺說不是官
不隱銀錢不現成小兒說
官無銀錢鄉紳有鄉紳為何
不出首爺娘說鄉紳有錢皀
已用那裏肯向學堂送小
兒說哎呀呀中國百姓外
國欺欺來去要分離那時
鄉紳做不成鄉紳為何不勤
心
齋健隆製

Long robes, mandarin jackets and pigtails were typical dressing image of Qing Dynasty's common men. The human figure in the left of the picture who wears a bowler hat was considered a "new style man" under the influence of so-called western civilization. (A New Year picture produced in Yanliuqing, Tianjin, collected by Wang Shucun)

the hair buns and wear hair decorations made by fur in winter, which had the double functions of keeping out the cold and decorating the hair. Women from the South liked to stick a delicate patterned wooden comb into hair horizontally. They often wore headscarves to shelter them from sunshine and wind, and head hoops in cold weather – a kind of head ornaments made by black velour or black satin that was wrapped around the head and tied at the back of the head with bands.

The Han women started to bind their feet when they were four or five years old. Except those who were engaged in hard labor work, women with big feet couldn't find someone to marry no matter whether they were from noble or plebeian families. The undesirable custom of footbinding started as early as in the Song Dynasty. Small and pointed feet were considered to be the essential qualifications of a beautiful woman.

Till the end of the Qing Dynasty, people with insight founded "No Footbinding Organization" in different provinces one after another. Under this movement of women liberation, women's feet were gradually set free.

Maybe because Manchu people used to live a kind of nomadic life, Manchu people in the Qing Dynasty liked to gird many daily articles for use. Men carried glasses case, fan covers, snuff boxes, pipes, flint, moneybags, little walking sabers etc. around waist. Women also liked to carry small daily articles. They didn't always tie them around the belt, but girded strands of articles in the front piece of the garment, such as a toothpick, nipper and earpick etc. Some women even carried more than ten pieces. Besides, they wore strands of flowers or handkerchiefs. More than that, they also wore all kinds of jewelry, such as earrings, arm bracelets, bracelets, finger rings, neck rings, bead strands made by gold, silver or jade. Even women from poor families liked to wear several pieces of silver ornaments.

Civilized New Clothes and Improved Cheong-sam

Marked by the Opium War that broke in1840, China entered the modern society. Strong warships and powerful cannons broke into the door of this ancient oriental country and brought in the western life styles and values. In the aspect of costume, the most distinct change was to cut pigtail and change clothes, which was advocated by those who had overseas study experience. Especially the "cut pigtail order" issued at the beginning of the founding of Republic of China (1911-1949) finally liberated Chinese men from heavy shameful pigtails. Some unprecedented changes appeared in Chinese dress history signified by all kinds of new style clothing that represented civilization and social development.

During the Republic of China Period, influenced by European and American fashion culture, the styles and forms of traditional Qing costumes gradually changed. Men from middle and upper class also wore Sun Yat-sen's

"A fashionable young lady" at the beginning of Republic of China Period. (Selected from the New Year picture with the same title, collected by Wang Shucun)

The young ladies in the picture wear "big garment piece" style coats with tight waistline and skirts. These were the so-called civilized new dresses. (Collected by Wang Shucun)

A traditional tailor shop in 1910s and 1920s. (Provided by Lu Zhongmin)

A traditional shoes shop in 1910s and 1920s. (Provided by Lu Zhongmin)

A short coat with round shape lower hem from the Republic of China Period. (Photo by Jin Baoyuan)

uniforms, western-style clothes, leather shoes, bowler hats besides long robes, mandarin jackets, cotton cloth shoes and skullcaps. Men in the streets wore cotton cloth long robes (mainly blue and grey color), short skirts and trousers made by locally produced white cotton cloth, cotton robes, tight cotton coats, cotton waistcoats and trousers with loose crotch and waistline. Ladies and girls from middle and upper class wore cheong-sams made by all kinds of outside materials, western style skirts, high-heel shoes and jewelry including gold, silver, jade and emerald. Women from lower class wore Chinese style jackets and coats made by patterned cotton cloth and embroidered shoes.

New styles and clothing arrangements appeared based on the Qing Dynasty men's daily robes and jackets. The mandarin jacket was *duijin* style down to the belly with tight sleeves, five buttons in the front garment piece. The long robe was usually "button to the right" style with big garment pieces and two inches above the ankle. On both sides of the robe, there were vents of about one "chi" (a meter=3 chi) long. The length of the sleeve was about the same as the length of jacket. Long robes and waistcoats going with western trousers, western style bowler hats, white scarves and shining leather shoes, this dressing style

Photo 1

Cheong-sams vary in the sleeve length, clothes body length and the width of the waistline. From these four cheong-sams, one can see the changes that cheong-sam experienced during the 1920s and 1930s. (Photo by Jin Baoyuan)

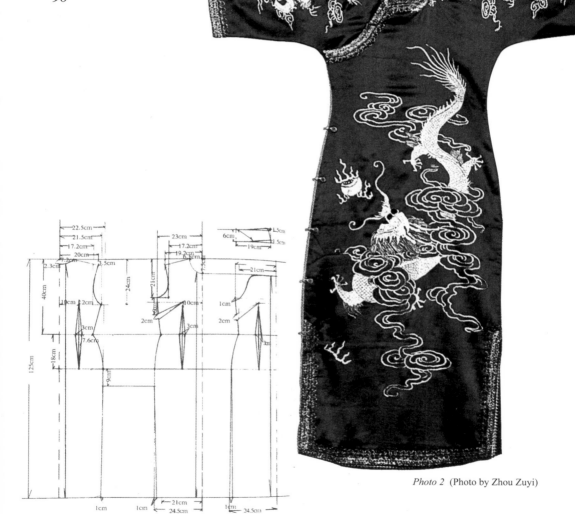

Photo 2 (Photo by Zhou Zuyi)

(**left**) *A cut-out plan for the cheong-sam of 1930s.*
(Provided by Zang Yingchun)

of combining Chinese and western clothes was the typical dress for middle and upper class men in early years of Republic of China. Wearing western suits completely were considered to be very a bold action.

In early years of Republic of China, many young students went to study in Japan, and brought Japanese student uniforms back. This clothing style that followed the western three-piece tailor with separate sleeves and clothes body cut showed a touch of youthful spirit, sobriety and refinement. It usually didn't use turndown collars, but narrow and low turn-up collars without ties or cravats. In the bottom part of the front garment piece, there were two hidden pockets on left and right sides. There was an outside-attached pocket in the left chest part. This student uniform was not only welcomed by many advanced young men but also transformed into the typical modern Chinese men's uniform – Sun Yat-sen's uniform.

Photo 4 (Photo by Zhou Zuyi)

The special features of Sun Yat-sen's uniforms are in the design of collars and pockets. A turn-up collar of fitted height plus a reverse collar has the effect of the wing collar of the western style skirt. There are four out pockets in the front garment piece. The lower two ones are pressed and tucked into the style of "qin pocket," so that more staff can be held. Soft covers are designed above the pocket to prevent articles from losing. There are two big hidden pockets inside the front garment underlining, a small one (watch pocket) in front of the waist and two on the behind with soft covers. This set of men's suit designed by the founder of Republic of China, Mr. Sun Yat-sen, is more practical than western suits, and fits more to the aesthetics and life customs of Chinese people. Even though it adopted the western cut, materials and color, but showed the qualities of the symmetry, solemnity and restraint of

Photo 3 (Photo by Zhou Zuyi)

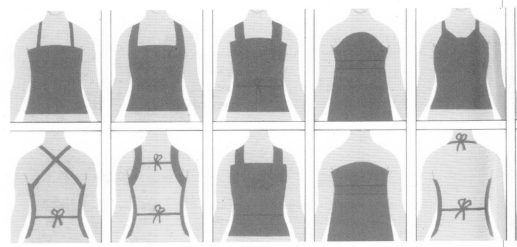

An evolution chart of women's underclothes in past dynasties. (Drawn by Gao Chunming, selected from Lady Garments and Adornments of Chinese Past Dynasties *written by Zhou Xun and Gao Chunming)*

Chinese dress. Since it came into being in 1923, the Sun Yat-sen's uniform has become the prevailing classical formal dress for Chinese men.

With the burst of the First World War, western feminist movement began to sprout. Women were no longer reconciled to be the accessories and victims of the family, so quite a number of women tried to pursue a career that had been previously occupied by men. They began to wear long trousers and cut short hair. This social tide converged with Chinese "New Civilization Movement" that had spread across China. Under these social influences of seeking for science, democracy and freedom, numerous women started to walk out of the family to receive higher education. They sought for both financial independence and freedom in love and marriage.

Female students who studied overseas and students from local mission schools took the lead in wearing "civilized new dress" – upper outer jacket was mostly jackets with tight waistline, big front garment pieces, elbow-long sleeves or 70% sleeves in the shape of horn.

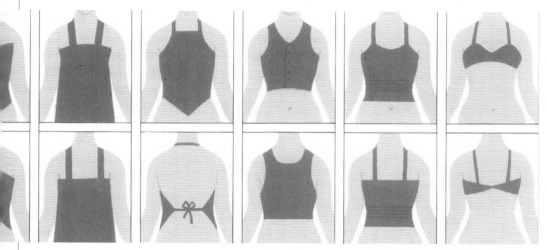

The clothing hem was mostly in arch shape and decorated with patterns. The matching skirts originally were ankle-long black skirts, and gradually the length of skirt rose to the upper shank. This style of simple and plain dress became the most fashionable female image in 1920s and 1930s. The esteem towards the western aesthetics also influenced the remoulding of the general image of Chinese women. Cosmetics and adornments from Europe and America entered into Chinese market. To whiten the skin, nourish hair, curl the eyelash, sweep dark eye shadow, cut short hair, curl hair, wear a Chanel style camellia or a very long pearl necklace around neck, carry a fur handbag, wear stockings and high heel shoes …these formed the daily images of Chinese fashionable women.

And the cheong-sam that is well received nowadays was also amended and improved in this period and became a modern fashionable dress.

The cheong-sam in Chinese is called "flag robe," which means the flag people's robe. And the flag people are how the middle land Han people referred to Manchu people. Possibly influenced by "Men and women are equal" thought, women who traditionally wore two-piece dress also wanted to follow men's one-piece dress style. In 1921, a group of female high school students in Shanghai took the lead to wear long robes. At the beginning, the prevailing style was a kind of blue cotton cloth cheong-sam with loose clothes body, straight and flat outline and bell-mouthed sleeves. The robe was ankle-long with no edgings or lacework in collar, front garment piece and hem parts. The robe looked very serious and formal. This style of dress aroused great interests of city women and was the rage once it appeared on the streets. Later under constant influences of modern tide, the cheong-sam showed changes in length, waistline, collars and sleeves.

In middle years of 1920s, the clothes body and sleeve of cheong-sams shortened, and the oxter part tightened. The robes were still decorated with embroidery and patterns. At the end of 1920s, the length of the robe shortened greatly, rising from the foot to ankle and then to the middle part of shank. The waistline tightened and the vents on both sides of the thigh part heightened also. After 1930s, cheong-sam improved and changed constantly. First high stand-up collar style was the rage, and then when it was high to reach the cheeks, low collar style began to prevail. When the collar couldn't be lower anymore, suddenly it was again heightened to look fashionable. The design of sleeves was the same case. It rose from wrist, to the middle of lower part of arm, to elbow, to the middle of the upper part of arm, and then finally there were no sleeves. The lower hem of robes sometimes was long enough to reach floor and sometimes was knee-high. Besides the vents on the sides, there might be a vent designed in the front garment piece and the lower hem was in the shape of arch. In terms of materials, besides the traditional jacquard woven brocade, more light and thin fabrics with printing such as cotton cloth, linen and silk were used. The colors chosen were usually simple but elegant. The collars, sleeves and garment pieces were decorated with edgings, but didn't look complicate with trivial details. Traditional Chinese costumes didn't highlight the waistline, but with the more and more distinct tendency of seeking the curve beauty of body shape in lady costumes, cheong-sams have become the most desirable dress to show the sexual body shape of women.

The style of cheong-sam in 1930s. (Provided by Hua Mei)

"A fashionable young lady" II. (Selected from the New Year picture with the same title, collected by Wang Shucun)

Farmer & Worker Uniforms
and Service-dresses

People's Republic of China was founded in 1949. In early years of new China, the so-called "bourgeois life style" was criticized which involved clothes and dressing styles. In those seaside cities that had been semi-colonized, some town folks who were influenced by western dress custom tended to wear western suits, leather shoes, cheong-sam and high-heel shoes. In most other cities, people still wore traditional long robes and mandarin jackets. Because political propaganda was so deeply rooted among people, though not stipulated by written order, western suits, cheong-sams, long robes and mandarin jackets were all considered to be the scum of the old society and abandoned by farmers and workers. The social etiquette also changed from bow to handshake or salute. The dresses of farmers and workers became the new fashion – overalls with gallus, working caps with a round top and front brim, cotton cloth rubber sole shoes, white head wrapping

This group photo shows the style and trend of men's wear in 1960s.

A peasant could also afford a sheep skin robe (Photographed in 1950, provided by Xinhua News Agency photo department)

towels, felt hats or straw hats, Chinese style short coats and loose trousers and square opening black cloth cover shoes etc. became signs of this new fashion. Even though sometimes there might be some improvements on the dress, they were hardly more than a turn-down collar and some outer pockets for the working dress. City women, however, wore printing cloth cotton coat of all different colors inside the blue or grey jackets. In festive days, the typical costume for Shan Bei Yangge (a popular rural folk dance) was to tie fresh red and green color ribbons around waist with two hands holding the two ends of the ribbon. The image of ribbons floating while dancing became the fad all over the country overnight.

The winter clothes for the workers in Northeast China. Long and short cotton padded coats were indispensable. (Photographed in 1956, provided by Xinhua News Agency photo department)

So there appeared some uniform dressing styles and typical dresses that were prevalent to an astonishing degree, such as the Lenin dress and patterned cotton coat which could represent this tendency. In early years of new P. R. China, Sino-Soviet Union relationship was close, so in China you could also see men wearing cricketcap – Soviet Union's worker's cap, and women wearing the Lenin dress. The so-called "Lenin dress" is a kind of diamond cloth double-breasted suit with a straight collar and sometimes with a cotton belt of the same color and two hidden pockets in the middle of lower part of front garment piece. Actually Lenin dress originally was not Soviet Union women's dress. Soviet Union women as well as other women in East Europe mostly wore skirts. Because it signified agricultural and industrial revolution, Lenin dress became the new dress style that symbolized the national renascence. Because its design was new and it could show the wearer's advanced thoughts, Lenin dress became the typical dress for governmental unit's female working staff.

Figured cloth cotton coat was also a sign of farmer and worker dress. Historically, this dress was the most common winter clothes for Chinese women and it has a long history. But in new China, the dressing way of figured cotton coat carried revolutionary meaning. Cotton coats made by scattered small flower patterned cloth of bold colors (mostly with red) were mainly the winter clothes for girls or young girls before 1950s. Adult women mostly used silk or satin as the surface materials of

98

the cotton coat. Women from poor family used plain color cloth. After the foundering of new China, traditional Chinese fabrics such as silk or satin seemed to carry strong feudalistic sense, so working women or female students abandoned satin and used flower pattern cloth to make their cotton coat to show their nearness to farmers and workers.

Women wore an unlined garment outside the cotton coat to prevent the coat from getting dirty and to avoid the frequent washing while maintaining the progressive image. In 1950s, those women who still had not walked out of home and started to work in the society were generally called housewife. These women didn't have strong consciousness of "women liberation," so over-clothes they wore were mostly in *duijin* style with knot buttons and *dajin* style for middle aged and old women. Most of the governmental department working staff, female workers and students wore Lenin dress as over-clothes. In the later years of 1960s, along with the deterioration of Sino-Soviet Union relationship, women no longer wore Lenin dress, but wore "welcoming guest dress." This dress was similar to men's Sun Yat-sen's uniform with a turn-down collar

Before 1980s, many housewives made clothes for their kids by themselves. The flowered cloth cotton padded coats worn by the mother and daughter in the picture were very popular style at that time. (Photographed in 1957, provided by Xinhua News Agency photo department)

and five buttons except some changes in collar and pocket design. This so called "welcoming guest dress" was very common in the decade between middle 1960s and middle 1970s. This dress was gradually abandoned when China adopted Reform and Open Door policy, but it was still very common among middle aged and old women until the middle and later part of 1990s.

No matter how style changed, those over clothes worn outside the flower patterned cotton coat were mostly solid color blue and grey, and some were brown and black. Women by nature love beautiful things, and would not bear wearing dark color dress for long period of time. So sometimes they would intentionally make the flower patterned cotton coat longer than the over clothes, and in this way, color and design of the cotton coat would be exposed in collar, sleeve and the lower

Beidaihe Beach in 1960s, people enjoying their vacation. (Photographed in 1961, provided by Xinhua News Agency photo department)

hem part. Even though it was easy to dirty the cotton coat in this way, this dressing way still became a fashion followed by many women.

Because of the large population and the great influence on clothes from political force that esteems unification, whatever dress it is, once it became popular, it could easily be spread nationwide in an astonishing degree. Who would ever imagine that in 1960s, Chinese people, who occupies the one-fourth of the world population, would take service uniform as civil dress?

Though falling into the western style army uniform category, in specific form and style, the Chinese People's Liberation Army uniforms try to avoid the influence from the European and American, but tend to be more Soviet Union style. In 1950s, Land Army Officers wore big army caps and soldier wore ship-

Long plaits were popular among women in 1960s. (Photographed in 1961, provided by Xinhua News Agency photo department)

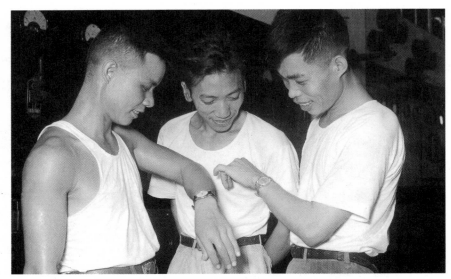

A watch used to be a luxury article in many Chinese people's life. (Photographed in 1957, provided by Xinhua News Agency photo department)

This was a clothes shop that made tailor-made clothes for customers. The tailor was helping the client to try on the clothes. (Photographed in 1961, provided by Xinhua News Agency photo department)

shaped caps. The collar type, tying way of the sam browne belt showed obvious features of Soviet Union army uniform. Navy uniforms adopted the standard international type. Officers wore big army caps, navy blue army uniforms in winter and white hats, white jackets, blue trousers in summer. Soldiers wore brimless army caps with two black ribbons hanging

Two children wearing the marine style kids clothes. (Photographed in 1955, provided by Xinhua News Agency photo department)

behind, white jackets with big turn-down collars in blue strips, blue trousers that were tied outside the jacket with brown cowhide belts. Because this kind of international standard marine uniform looked nice, for long period of time, there was a type of children's clothes that imitated the uniform. But for children, the army caps with hard tops were replaced with brimless caps with soft tops, and words of "Chinese People's Liberation Army" around the cap were replaced with "Chinese People's Young Navy." This type of dress was generally called "navy uniform." But other land army and air service uniforms were not popular among common people.

In 1965, the standing committee of Chinese National People's Congress decided to abolish the military mark system, and the corresponding change was that both officers and soldiers all wore liberation caps with a round top and front brim on which a metal red pentagram shape badge was attached. Army jackets had five buttons and a stand collar on which a red flag badge was sewn at the two ends of collar. The army uniform had no shoulder mark or arm badge or any kind of military marks. The differences between officer and soldier uniform were the materials and the pocket design. For officers above main platoon rank, uniforms used wool-dacron textile and there were four pockets in the front garment piece. Those under the rank of vice platoon were treated as soldiers. Their uniform used cotton textile and there

Before the popularization of washing machines in Chinese families, people usually used clothes scrubbing boards made of wood or plastic to wash their clothes. (Photographed in 1973, provided by Xinhua News Agency photo department)

were only two upper pockets. There were no army type skirts and brimless caps for female soldiers and their uniform style was similar to male soldiers' uniform. The color for land army uniform was olive green, for air force was green for upper clothes and blue for pants and for navy was grey. The stand collar uniform jacket of three armies was generally called "service dress" (There was no full dress at that time) and the most typical army green was the dominant color.

Since Cultural Revolution (1966-1976) began, the image of liberation army uniform had become the most revolutionary, pure and reliable symbol. The trend started with army men's children turning out their father's uniform and soon the image of green army

Small flower patterned cotton cloth overcoats were very popular in 1950s and 1960s. (Photographed in 1955, provided by Xinhua News Agency photo department)

uniform with brown leather belt became to lead the trend. Following that, universities and high schools all over the country one after another founded the "Red Guard" organization; primary schools founded "Little Red Guard" organization, and workers and farmers started to set up "Red Guard Team." Everyone was supposed to take the responsibility of a soldier. Because they couldn't find the true uniforms, Red Guards then bought the army uniform reproductions, which were generally called the service dress. Without the cap badge, collar badge and shoulder badge, red guards used a red sleeve badge printed with yellow color character of "Red Guard" to show their status.

The decade before the new China, traffic policemen's winter uniforms were blue "big crown" caps, blue jackets and blue trousers. Those on shift wore white raglan sleeve that reached shoulder. Summer uniforms were white "big crown" caps, white jackets and blue trousers. When cultural revolution raged tempestuously, policemen's uniforms completely copied the army uniforms – the color changed into green, the "big crown" cap changed into the cloth liberation cap with a round top, and black leather shoes changed into green rubber sole cloth shoes. To differ it from the red pentagon army badge, policemen still wore their policeman badge in front of the cap.

It was the "going up to mountain and down to countryside" movement participated by 30 million city young people that pushed "service dress rage" to another climax. In 1964, the first bunch of young intellectual young men hurried to Xinjiang to reclaim the wasteland and founded Xinjiang Production and Construction Corps. When they were seen off at the train station, they wore green service dresses and military caps, but without cap badges and collar badges. In 1968, large scale of young intellectuals "going up to mountain and down to countryside" movement began, they all wore green service dresses dispatched by the nation when they hurried to countryside or remote places.

Another important form of "everyone taking the responsibility of a soldier" was the possemen's drill. The simulative army drill was rather common. Workers, intellectuals and school students were all proud of wearing army uniforms. Those who didn't wear service dress would wear blue or grey uniforms, but they still wore green army caps and rubber sole shoes and carried army marching pack bags, army satchels and kettles. This times of "everyone wearing army uniforms" gradually ended along with the advent of China's Reform and Opening Door policy.

In the middle and later period of 1980s, there was another round of "everyone wearing army uniform" trend – every winter, people of all classes, sexes, and social positions wore army cotton padded overcoats. Because that traffic vehicle was mainly bicycles in those times, indoor clothes were not suitable for outside cold weather and the newly arisen winter proofing coat was too short to cover the legs, the makeshift was to buy an inexpensive but practical army overcoat. Army overcoat became trendy dress.

This army dress trend lasted about ten years. Until the beginning of 1990s, when leather coats and down coats appeared in the market in large volume, army overcoats gradually faded from one's memory.

The special counter that sold printed cloth in Beijing Department Store in 1970s. (Photographed in 1974, provided by Xinhua News Agency photo department)

Professional Image and Professional Dresses

Professional dresses are the dresses that indicate the profession. In 1978, China began to reform and open its door to outside world, all kinds of professional dresses which symbolized the image of professions emerged as the times required. For staff from many professions such as public security, traffic management, procuratorate, courthouse, post office, taxation service, industry and commerce, civil air force and railway, the nation designed, made, and dispatched professional dresses according to different professions. Professional dresses were made and dispatched by their own departments even for those professions that were difficult to set a national standard. Some schools not only bought student uniforms for students, but also tailor-made western style clothes for teachers.

The trend of wearing uniform had quickly spread since 1980s. Because the color and the style were rather

The uniforms of air attendants for Air China. (Provided by Imaginechina)

The national standard uniforms for Chinese policemen. (Provided by Imaginechina)

similar, it seemed that tipstaff are everywhere.

Professional dress is different from the normalized full dress, because it has the effect of showing identity, status and power, for example, the professional dress for manager and shop assistant are different in style and color. Generally speaking, once certain profession appears in certain dress image, it will be easily identified and recognized. When people think of this profession, first thing that comes into mind is the dressing image of this profession or when people see certain specific dressing image, they will instantly correspond it to its related profession. Postmen are called "messenger in green dress" and medical staffs are called "angles in white dress." So dress could display people's social character and social character enriches the cultural image of the professional dress.

The development level of commodity economy is closely related with the development of professional dress. As early as in the Song Dynasty, because city and town economy developed quickly, professional dress had already shown the necessity of dress socialization. It was recorded that "people who sell medicine and divinatory symbols all wear hats and belts and as for beggars, they also have dress

Skirts with suspenders as the major style for female students' summer school uniforms were popular for long time. (Photographed in 1954, provided by Xinhua News Agency photo department)

Worker caps used to be important professional dressing signs for workers, but seldom seen nowadays. (Photographed in 1961, provided by Xinhua News Agency photo department)

standards to follow." This standard that society created for professional dress in fact was the signs of social civilization. There were also the written descriptions for hotels and restaurants in old times, "women in neighborhood who tie blue and white cloth towels around waist and coil up wei hair bun, pour wine and exchange soup dishes for the guest." Obviously professional dresses in that time were categorized only by professions. Though a specific dressing image of certain restaurant had not formed, it actually possessed the basic features of professional dress.

In fact, the scope of professional dress is not

(**top**) *White-collar dresses are different for different professions.* (Provided by Imaginechina)
(**bottom**) *Western suits and ties are typical professional dresses for men who work in Lujiazui Financial Street in Shanghai.* (Provided by Imaginechina)

limited to uniforms. The specific dress for diplomatic conference, economic and trading negotiations, office, scientific research labs, schools and workshops of precise instrument, and the special dress for hotels, hostels, shops and traffic profession, or the dress for hard labored workers, such as cleaners, operating personnel and cargadors, all fall into to the scope of professional dress.

Professional dress that has the effect of identification could help to build the favorable professional image for certain profession or certain enterprises and good professional dress even has the brand effect. Along with the strengthening of the CI design consciousness, designers, the theoretical circle of clothes and even users all have realized the importance and promising future of the professional dress.

Since 1990s, along with China entering the commodity economy times, professional dress has had more extensive connotations. The importance of individuation and fashion is underlined in design. Besides the fixed professional dress for special professions, shirts, western trousers and ties seem to form a standard officer worker image. When attending formal occasions, men usually wear suits and leather shoes, which have become a social etiquette. Compared with men, professional women have more choices in terms of dressing style and clothing arrangement. While seeking more career space to develop, Chinese professional women have paid more and more attention to their outlooks. Many topics in media are stressing the meaning of using decent and fashionable dress to earn more favor for one's profession.

Adornments and Fairy Tales

Chinese minority costumes are famous for their vivid color, fine handicraft and rich varieties. The fact that they attach great importance to costume details is related with their nationalities' origin and history. Those patterns, design and adornments, which had been handed down for generations, are not only delicate handicrafts, but also extensions of the minority cultural traditions. People could taste the rich social meanings and explore the customs and taboos behind.

In southwest border area of China, there live the old De'ang ethnic group people. The most typical costume feature in De'ang costumes is the dozens of rattan hoops around girls' waist. It is said that the ancestors of De'ang came from gourd. Men all looked the same and women flew into the sky when they came out of gourd. It was the god of heaven who differentiated the facial features of men and helped men to catch women. The god tied women with rattan

The traditional phoenix dress for women of She minority. (Painted by Li Ling)

(top) *In Liuzhi special zone in Guizhou there lives a branch of Miao minority- Long Horn Miao. One of the smallest Chinese nationality branches, its population is only over 6,000. For years living in the Daqing Mountain with an altitude of 1600 meters, they live an isolated primitive tribe style life. The head decorations for women are huge and heavy. They use an ox horn shape wood board of 1.5-2 chi (1 meter=3 chi) to coil their 3-6 kilos black hair to the back of their head into a huge "∞" shape on the wood horn. About 15 centimeters high, the head decorations come down below ears and above shoulders. Long horns represent the nationality's worship and hope toward nature.* (Photo by Chen Yinian, provided by image library of Hong Kong *Traveling in China*)

(bottom) *Tattoo is a kind of important aboriginal cultural feature and its patterns are mostly related closely with the primitive worship. This picture shows a Miao man with tattoos.* (Photo by Chen Yinian, provided by image library of Hong Kong *Traveling in China*)

hoops and women were no longer able to fly. Hence women started to live together with men and multiply for generations and generations.

The waist hoops are made by bamboo strips. Some use bamboo strips in front and screwy silver threads in the back. Waist hoops are in different width, painted with red, yellow, black and green color, carved with patterns or coated with silver cover. The more waist hoops people wear and the more delicate the handicraft, the more honorable they would feel. For two people in love, those waist hoops that are made with elaborate efforts could show the cleverness and deftness of the fancy man and the sincere love for the girls. The more waist hoops adult women wear and the higher the grade of the material, the stronger their husbands' commercial power is and the higher is her position in the family.

The waist decorations of Yi women are very unique. The style is not beautiful and soft, but rather rugged. Yi women traditionally wear big black waist rings usually made of elm tree skin. There is a legend about its origin. When Yi people in ancient times encountered their enemies, women ran for battlefield together with men. They were brave and good at fighting and they often used waist rings with iron cover to protect themselves in battle. Later, Yi women were no longer involved in battle, but still kept the tradition of using black waist rings for decoration. They consider waist rings as a kind of protective talisman and lucky sign.

Va minority girls also like to wear waist hoops, which were made mainly by bamboo or rattan in the past. Only women from rich family would use strings of beads or black lacquer bamboo rings to make the hoop. Some girls from richer families even used silver waist rings decorated with patterns. Yi women decorate their upper arms and wrist with silver bracelets and some bamboo or rattan hoops on their thigh and shank.

The silver belt of Dai girls is considered to be very precious. Some are handed down from mother to daughter for many generations. But in daily life, a silver waist belt is considered to be the love sigh. If a girl gives the silver belt to a young guy, it means that she falls in love with him.

Mongolian people in North also have unique waist adornments. Whenever grassland parties come and the most traditional horse racing and wrestling contests are held, young men will wrap a kind of special wide leather belt or silk ribbon. In daily dress, waist belts are also an indispensable part. Some belts are made by leather, but most are made by cotton cloth or silk. The belt is about three to four meters

Waist loops worn by women of De'ang minority. (Painted by Li Ling)

long. Because Mongolians are the horseback minority who are engaged in stock herding and also because they live in cold and windy area, tying a belt will not only prevent wind and coldness, but also keep the stabilization of waist and backbone while riding horse and holding halter.

Men would lift up the robes when tying belt in order to facilitate riding. They carry Mongolian knifes, flint and cigarette holders on their waist belts. Women like to pull down the robe when tying waist ribbons to make the robe smooth, which would highlight waistline and the beauty and uprightness of the body. The waist belt outside the Ewenke herdsman's robe also has its own cultural connotations. It is considered to be a very impolite behavior for men and women not wearing waist belts. Women could tie no waist belt in usual time, but must tie belts when doing labor work. Yugur minority people who are engaged in stock farming also attach great importance to the waist belt. Men mostly wear red and blue belts, and hang waist knifes, steel for flint, flint, small wine kettles, snuffboxes or China tobacco pipes. Women mostly wear red, green or purple waist belts decorated with several colorful handkerchiefs sometimes. Russians in Northwest China like to wear thin waist belts made by leather or cotton, but mostly they wear silk belts woven by silk threads with a beautiful knot at the right side of the waistline and tassels hanging down naturally. Qiang people are good at embroidery. Besides using brocade waist belts, they also like to embroider colorful and fancy patterns on cloth waist belts.

All kinds of waist adornments attract modern anthropologists and fashion designers for their rich culture. Tracing back to the origin, waist adornments carry primitive life worship meaning, but for modern people who seek for change and arrangement aesthetics, waist decorations are only a kind of popular adornments.

If those people who have been to Zhejiang, Fujian, Guangdong and Jiangxi in China see the local She minority girls, they will definitely be attracted by the unique head adornment – "Phoenix Crown,"a kind of red round piece of head adornment stretched from the back to the forehead. Because red hair threads are interwoven with hair, the phoenix crown could also be considered as a kind of hairstyle. Married women's hairstyle is different. They comb their hair into high pail type hair bun, cover the back of the head with a chicken crest shape cap and bind red wool thread in hair. Some women put a 5cm or shorter bamboo pipe on top of the head and wrap their hair around the bamboo pipe into a whorl shape. They use tea oil or water to comb the hair and mix hair with fake hair, so their hair buns look tall, fluffy and lustrous. The "phoenix crown" for the bride is a kind of small and pointing cap made by bamboo pipes, covered by yellow cloth, and decorated with silver boards, bells and red cloth strips. Four pieces of red cloth strips hang down to the waist and a row of silver small human figures hang in front of the forehead to cover the face, which makes the bride look pretty and mysterious. In festive days, She minority people would wear the complete set of "phoenix dress," which not only shows remembrance to their ancestors, but also makes them feel the protection from the previous generations. This is the ancestor worship existing in the costumes. In Chinese costumes as well as costumes of all mankind, one could always see primitive worship cultural

A mask used in ceremonial dance performed by the Lamaists in exorcism in Taer Temple in Qinghai Province. (Photo by Cai Xingmin, provided by image library of Hong Kong *Traveling in China*)

This is a kind of clothing material used often among local women of minorities in Guizhou Province – batik. They paint the wax liquid to the white cloth according to patterns using special copper wax knife, dip and dye the cloth in indigo after wax gets dried. Then they boil off the wax with boiling water after the cloth is dry. In this way, the cloth will create all kinds of beautiful blue and white patterns because the part with wax is not dyed due to the protection of wax. The part with protection wax will create ice-cracking pattern because some indigo will seep into the cracking. This is a piece of batik work of peacock pattern. (Photo by He Huaibo provided by image library of Hong Kong *Traveling in China*))

concept displayed in all kinds of forms, either in general costume images or just a detail.

Legend says that the ancestor of She minority was Pan Hu King. Because of his great contributions on fighting off the enemies, he became the daughter-in-law of the headman of the tribe and married the third princess. At the wedding day of Pan Hu King, the bride's mother gave his daughter a very precious phoenix crown and a phoenix dress decorated with jewels to show her bless to her daughter. After marriage, she gave birth to three sons and one daughter and lived happily. When her daughter got married, beautiful and elegant phoenix magically flew out of mountain (hence this mountain was named Phoenix Mountain, located inside the Guangdong Province now), holding in mouth a very colorful and fancy phoenix dress. Since then, She women have been considering phoenix dress as the most beautiful holy dress that could bring them luck and safety.

The phoenix dress nowadays is embroidered with

red, peach red or yellow patterns and more delicate ones are embroidered with gold or silver threads to represent the fancy feathers of phoenixes. The phoenix crown represents the exalted phoenix head. Because phoenixes are the musicians in the fairy world who understand music, phoenix dresses will be covered with tinkly silver adornments, representing the singing of the phoenix.

Yi minority people, who live in the Small and Big Liang Mountain, have unique costumes with a long history. Yi People worship leather loricae, because they believe loricae could protect the safety of family and individual. It was said that ancient people used rhinoceros skin and elephant skin to make loricae, and what we could see now are mainly made by cattle skin with rawhide as the roughcast. They are coated with lacquer and decorated with colorful lacquer pattern. The animal patterns used are dragon and python surrounded with arrowheads and the edge decoration is clouds. The implied meaning is that dragon and python are the animals sent to the human world by deity to help the loricae's owner to conquer enemies. They could protect loricae wearer's safety and help them win the victory by shielding lance and arrows. Among Yi people, they divide the loricae into two types: male and female. The color of male loricae is mainly red while the color of female loricae is black. In Yi 's other artworks, they also like to use black, red and yellow colors. Black color signifies sobriety, red signifies courage and passion, and yellow signifies beauty and brightness. Yi people worship black, military force and respect fire, which are well displayed in their leather loricae.

Dai women like to embroider peacock pattern on

their costumes. Besides showing their remembrance to their ancestors, they believe that peacocks could bring luck to Dai People. A long Dai poem describes the story of a beautiful and kind peacock princess who flies into the lake to bath one day. A prince who was deeply in love with her took her peacock dress away. The prince hoped that in this way he could keep the peacock princess. Later they fell in love, and then got married and lived happily. The peacock king got irritated after knowing this and sent troops to go on a punitive expedition. The prince led soldiers to meet the attack, but the prince's father believed in slanderous talk and planed to kill the peacock princess. The princess requested to dance with the peacock dress before her death but took this chance to fly away. The prince prayed for the help of magic dragon and crossed mountains, rivers and oceans to reunite with his princess. To commemorate this lovely couple, Dai people started to wear peacock clothes during festival days or embroider the peacock pattern on their

Horn crown decorations are very commonly seen in Miao area. The silver decoration can be as long as almost half of the body height. These adornments are very beautiful, delicate and with strong flavor of primitive worship. (Photo by Chen Yinian provided by image library of Hong Kong *Traveling in China*)

costumes. People dance together to display Dai people's supplication to beauty and happiness.

Men of Yao minority who live in Guangxi wear white trousers. These are not plain white trousers, but decorated with five or seven strips of red cloth on the knee part and some are embroidered with red threads and decorated with small patterns of all different shapes. This practice of sewing red cloth on white trousers also came from a very touching ancestor worship story. Long long ago, their ancestors lived and worked in peace and contentment, but suddenly there came a demon who asked people to present their food supplies and girls and also take orders from him. A handsome and brave young guy in the tribe led his tribe people to fight with the demon. He took the lead in chasing the demon into a mountain. When people arrived, they found the young guy had already perished together with the demon. In his hands, he still seized the demon's hair. Bloodstain scratched by the demon's big paws was left on his clothes. To recall this hero who drove away the evil demon for the people, Yao people began to embroider or sew red vertical stripes pattern on their white trousers to signify the blood mark scratched by the demon, to commemorate the ancestor and to spirit up themselves.

Hats with Meanings

In the thick forest of the Grand and Small Xing An Moutain in China, there live E'lunchun people who use animal fur to make clothes for generations. Elunchun people's clothes are almost all made of roe fur. In autumn and winter, they use roe captured in autumn and winter, which has a stronger winter-proofing capacity because of its long and thick fur hair and thick and strong skin. Roe fur worn in summer use roes captured in summer because of its thin and short fur hair.

Roe fur clothes of Elunchun people include roe robes, coats, trousers, boots, socks, gloves, aprons, waistcoats, and even satchels. These are all made of roe fur. Among these fur clothes, the most characteristic one is the roe head hat. A roe head hat is made by a piece of complete roe head fur. The traditional way is first to peel off the skin from the roe head and the head fur was then coated with animal liver smashed into

Head scarves of Miao people in the east part of Guizhou and west part of Hunan. People must master the scarf-wrapping skill when they reach the age of 12 or 13. The length of scarf ranges from 4 or 5 meters to more than 10 meters. They wrap the scarf into a pail shape in layers and consider high "scarf hat" as beautiful and unique. (Photo by Chen Yinian provided by image library of Hong Kong Traveling in China)

In middle land of China, there is a tradition of using the figure of tiger to decorate kids including tiger hats, tiger shoes, tiger toys and even tiger pillows. The picture shows the common "tiger hat" for kids. (Photographed in 1950, provided by Xinhua News Agency photo department)

mushy paste or deadwood dregs mixed with water after being dried. Then the fur is rolled up and covered tightly for one or two days to soften and ferment the adhesive materials like fat on the skin. The decayed stuff was then scraped off and the fur is kneaded repeatedly until the fur softens. Two black pieces of leather skin are sewed to the eye socket parts as eyes. Two ears were sliced off and replaced by two fake ears made by roe skin. In this way, a lifelike roe head hat is finished. Using fake ears for the roe head hat is to meet the needs of hunting – a roe head hat is the best camouflage for hunting. When a hunter hides in the forest with only roe head hat being exposed, wild roes often drop their guard because they consider him as their same kind. Hence it is easy for hunters to hunt for prey when they enter into their field of vision. If a roe head hat uses real ears, then other hunters will be confused, which may cause shots by accident.

Daur people who live in the northeast of China also love to use animal fur to make fur hats. Besides roe heads, they also use fox and wolf fur to make hats. Ewenke people who have been living in rich forest, grassland and valley south of the Erguna River in northeast China for generations also wear beast head hats. Besides using roe heads, they also use the fur of Mongolian dog and deer. The style is rugged and lifelike. Using real animal heads to make animal head hats could be considered a typical costume feature among northeast nomadic nationalities, which is closely related with their commercial activity.

Occupying the highest position in general costume image, hats that well display the costume culture are paid particular attention. Some hats record the origin of their nationalities; some display the intelligence of their people; some concern the local weathers; and some signify the social position or commercial conditions of their wearers. Generally speaking, people exert great

The unique head decoration for women of Yao minority in Guoshan area in Guangxi Province. (Photo by Chen Yinian provided by image library of Hong Kong *Traveling in China*)

artistic talent on the design of hats. Whatever it displays, beauty is never neglected.

A Yugur felt hat is like an inverted horn. The horn opening extents outward to form a circle of round hat brim decorated with two rings of black silk ribbons. The horn mouth forms the hat crown. The crown is decorated with all kinds of patterns and unique red tassels. It is said that this type of hat is to commemorate a female hero in Yugur minority's history. For the happiness of their people, she fought to the last blood against the devils. Red tassels in Yugur's hats signify her fresh blood.

Yi girls who inhabit in the Red River area in Yunnan all have their cherished cockscomb hats. It is said that a loving couple fought against devils holding torches high, in order to seek for happiness and brightness and save country fellow from darkness. But unfortunately they fell into devil's hands. Later, the girl escaped cleverly with the help of an old man. The old man taught her to make a cock to crow in order to call the sun out. The devils were then drive away. The girl saved her boyfriend and their country fellow also saw the brightness. In order to show their gratitude for the cock that saved their life, Yi people started to make cockscomb and put them on girls' heads because they believe that cock could bring luckiness, brightness, safety and happiness to the world. Besides Yi minority, Hani minority and Bai Minority girls in Yunnan also like to wear cockscombs of similar shapes and styles.

There is a legend about kirgiz' hats. In ancient time, there was a brave and sagacious king. He realized that in the battle, their national army troops were disorderly and unsystematic and hardly to be recognized because of their inconsistent clothes and hats. So he summoned all departments and ordered them to design a kind of unified hat for soldiers within 40 days. This hat should look like a shining star, a colorful flower, an ice peak covered with snow and a mountain slope covered with thick grass. It should be able to shield rain, snow, wind and sand. 39 days passed, nobody could design a kind of hat that satisfied both the king and the people. On the 40th day, the beautiful daughter of a royal

The hat and dress of Hani minority in Yunnan Province. (Photo by Wu Jialin provided by image library of Hong Kong *Traveling in China*)

consultant designed a decorative white felt hat. The king was very satisfied and ordered both his army and people to wear this kind of hat, which since then has been handed down for generations until now. This kind of hat is made of wool felt and in the shape of coiled eaves with either flat crown or spire crown of four ridges. There is a vent on both sides of the hat brim, which divide the hat brim into front and back part. If all brims are rolled to the top, the hat could shield snow and rain. If only the front brim is let down, the hat could shade the sunshine. And if both front and back brims are let down, the hat could shield wind and sand. Kirgizs consider this kind of hat as sacred hats. They hang them in high places or places not easily to be accessed when not wearing them. One could not throw or trample the hats or make joke on them, which were considered to be ill omened.

Mongolian noble women in ancient time wore a kind of high and big hat crown, and later these hats were not limited to noble women anymore. In festive days or big celebrations, women from ordinary families also wore this kind of hat. The hat crown is enclosed with birch skin, 30-50cm high and quadrangle shape at the top. The hat is covered with colorful silk and decorated with bead pieces, amber, peacock feathers or blackcock feathers etc. Any other adornments on the hat could be added or deleted at will, but feathers could not be

Women in Huian area in Fujian Province wear yellow bamboo hats and flower pattern head scarves. The bamboo hat is painted with yellow paint to prevent against the sunshine and rain. The scarf is square, and has small green or blue flowers on white background or white flowers on green or blue background. It is folded into triangle shape and wrapped around head to prevent against the wind and sand, to keep warm and protect the hairstyle. (Photo by Wang Miao provided by image library of Hong Kong Traveling in China)

omitted. Besides, girls also like to wrap a scarf around head, usually using cloth or silk of more than one meter long. The wrapping ways are different in different areas and for people of different ages.

Those nationalities that believe in Islam and Orthodox Church attach great importance to hats. Indeed they wear hats everyday, because according to the doctrine walking outside without wearing hats is profane to the heaven and disrespectful to the older members of the family. The Hui minority people mainly wear white cloth brimless little round hats. Together with black cloth hats, these two types of hats are considered to be "chapel hats" – hats that they wear when going chapels. Because there are different sects of the religion, there are hats in the shape of pentagon, hexagon and octagon and even there is a kind of hard helmet hat. Veils and scarves of women also differ in different sects of religion, area and age. Thus we could see that costumes are related with culture. Especially head costumes are always directly related with religious beliefs.

Uygur in Xinjiang Autonomous Region mostly believe in Islam. More common than Hui Minority, Uygur, no matter what ages and sexes, almost all wear hats. Looking very beautiful, Uygur's little hats are decorated with delicate patterns and in big varieties. Besides, there are many rules on how to wear the hats. According to the different area, sex, age and occasion, they would wear different types of patterned hats. We could say that Uygur's patterned hats are as famous as their song and dance. Hats are not only their daily articles, but also a kind of traditional handicraft. There are many types of patterned hats and all patterns are beautifully designed. Some are simple but elegant with white flowers in dark backgrounds. Some are complicated and fancy with patterns of little birds intertwining with flowers. Some have several rings of little flowers around hats and the most fancy ones are decorated with flower patterns made by gold, silver threads, beads and tassels.

Two Mongolian hunters wearing animal skin hats in winter snow. (Photo by Ebo provided by image library of Hong Kong *Traveling in China*)

Shawls and the Back Wrapping Cloth

The "Wearing stars and moons" or "Seven stars shawl" indicates the lambskin shawl of Naxi women. It is usually made by a complete piece of lambskin and sewed with black wool cloth edgings of 6 cm wide. At the two shoulder parts, two round plates are embroidered using silk threads to signify the sun and moon. Underneath, there is a row of seven small round plates that signify the stars. The complete shawl is tied in front of the chest using wide white cloth ribbon.

Besides Naxi women, other nationalities also have all kinds of shawls. In Yi minority area in Yunnan Province, women like to wear a kind of unique costume – back wrapping cloth, which has the similar function as the "wearing stars and moons." While carrying big bamboo baskets or heavy things to climb mountains, they could use it to prevent hard and heavy baskets to

The dress image of women of Drung minority. (Painted by Li Ling)

A Ming Dynasty woman wearing a cloud patterned shawl. (Part of the Painting *Sixty Beauties* by Ming Dynasty painter Chou Ying)

h u r t
the waist.
Even when not
carrying heavy
things, back wrapping
cloth also could keep the
waist part warm. When having

A material object of Qing Dynasty tippet with colored embroidery and cloud pattern. (Photo by Zhou Zuyi)

a rest while doing labor work, it can be used as a cushion to sit. Yi minority's back wrapping cloth is different from Naxi's sheepskin shawl in its size, which is relatively small with a diameter of 25cm and thickness of 1 cm. It is not made of the complete sheepskin, but a piece of round wool felt. Embroidered tying ribbons of around 2 meters long are tacked on the back wrapping cloths. The tying ribbons intersect in front of chest, and back wrapping cloth hang down the back to cover the waist and the behind. In terms of style and way of doing, there are two types of back wrapping cloth: one is traditional, with its surface not covered with cloth cover, but embroidered with patterns of two bronze drum halo lines and two horizontal rectangular. The patterns are usually black dotted with some red and yellow color, which shows a simple and rugged style. For the other kind, its surface is covered with black cloth and embroidered with all kinds of delicate and beautiful patterns. A piece of back wrapping cloth draped at the back shines together with the colorful costumes, which forms the typical clothing feature of Yi women in the west part of Yunnan.

There is a beautiful legend that talks about the adornments of the back wrapping cloth. It is said that long time ago, several Yi girls who were chased by army soldiers hid themselves in the Qinghua cave in the east part of Dali in the turmoil of war.

A traditional embroidered shawl. (Provided by image library of Hong Kong *Traveling in China*)

The "back wrapping cloth" for women of Naxi minority. (Photo by Li Zhixiong, provided by image library of Hong Kong *Traveling in China*)

While girls were feeling scared, several spiders came out and wove a web on the cave opening. When chasing soldiers arrived to check out, they figured out that there must be no people hidden inside and then left in a hurry because they saw the spider webs on the cave opening. After the girls escaped from the danger, they embroidered the spider on their felt in order to thank for the spider for saving their lives. This is how the pattern of two circles with a ring of closed angle lines came from. There is another kind of explanation that says that two circles are two open eyes. Wearing a piece of back wrapping cloth will add two more eyes at back, which could scare off the devils and the evils.

Moinba women who live in Men'ou area and Muotuo County have the tradition of draping a whole piece of calfskin or goatskin at the back of their robes. Girls usually drape a piece of lambskin that still keeps its tail and four legs and ladies drape calf or goatskin pieces. Even in wedding ceremony, a bride in full dress would drape a piece of good lambskin. It is said that the Wencheng Princess (? - 680) in the Tang Dynasty once draped a piece of animal skin when she entered the Tibet area for the sake of keeping the evils away. When she passed by Men'ou Area, she gave this animal skin piece to a Moinba lady. This is obviously a legend about friendship and communication between different nationalities. The calf or lambskin pieces that they drape mainly have two functions. First, Men'ou's weather is very cold and wet, so carrying a piece of animal skin will keep the body warm, prevent against the moisture and shelter the wind and rain. Secondly, places they live are full of steep slopes and narrow roads, so it is easier to carry heavy things on back than on shoulder. The lambskin piece has the same function of "star and moon shawl" of Naxi and the back wrapping cloth of Yi people.

Yi women and men who live in Grand and Small Liang Mountain in Sichuan and Yunnan region all wear "caerwa," which is rather big with about the same size of a loose and big shawl. It is woven by linen and supplemented with wool. A Caerwa has many functions and is considered to be "a coat during day, a raincoat when rain comes and a quilt at night." Old men usually wear black and blue caerwas, while young men like to use flamboyant colors of strong contrast such as red, yellow, green, orange and pink. It was tied around neck at the top, opens in front and has tassels at the bottom. Men will look handsome, masculine and powerful when wearing caerwas and the "hero knot" on the head. Women will look pretty, elegant and rustic when they wear colorful caerwas, flower patterned head handkerchiefs together with a kind of hairstyle with two plaits crossing and wrapping around head top.

A sheepskin waistcoat of Qiang people opens in front without buttons. Though it is not a type of shawl clothing, basically it was also draped around shoulders. Qiang's sheepskin waistcoat is the symbolic costume of Qiang minority. People of all ages and sexes, even toddlers, will wear "Chu Feng" type fur waistcoats that are not face-covered. Outside is naked sheepskin. Edges are sewn into patterns or sewn neatly. "Chu Feng" means that fur expose outside from waistcoat edges at the parts of shoulder, front piece and lower hem. Qiang people call it "fur jacket." In sunny days, they will wear the waistcoat with naked sheepskin side being exposed outside and in rainy days the fur side being exposed, which will enable rain drop to flow down along with drooping fur. Same as the caerwa of Yi minority, it also has the function of coir raincoats. Qiang people also have a kind of brown and black thick woolen "Muzi" jacket of 1.5 meters long. Like a fur waistcoat, it not only helps to prevent against coldness, but also shelter rain. Whenever necessary, it can be used as a cushion or quilt. Besides, it can help to protect the back when carrying heavy things.

The costume that looks most natural and unstrained is the Drung minority's stripes linen cloth blanket. Because Drung people, no matter what age or sex, all drape this kind of linen blanket with very simple clothes arrangement inside, it has become the most characteristic costume. Drung people call it "Yuduo," while people not from their nationality usually call it the "Drung blanket." The way of draping the blanket looks about the same at first sight. They drape it around one shoulder and expose another shoulder, mostly left shoulder. But if categorizing carefully, there are many rules. Men wrap slantwise a linen blanket on the back from left axilla to right shoulder and tie them in front of the chest. Women drape two square blankets, from shoulder to the knee part. Blankets overlap either from left side or right side. If the blankets are wrapped to the right, the waist part is then tied tightly with ropes and blankets will cover both the front and back. If to the left, then it is more flexible to put on or take off.

Because the stripes of the Drung's blanket are arranged harmoniously in different width and colors are primitive and simple, people from other nationalities nearby also like to purchase to wear. However, it seems that they lack a special charm shown in Drung people. Both Drung women and men hang hair down loosely with eye-brow length hair bang hang in front of forehead. Hair at the back hangs down to the shoulder that covers ear tips. They wear big and round earrings, or insert bamboo sticks into their ear holes. In the past, Drung women usually tattoo their face by dipping black liquid made by pan dust onto their faces.

Costumes that were draped around shoulders are mostly adornments evolved gradually from labor work or life. They still keep the double functions of decoration and practical use. Unlike clothes that are usually worn neatly in set, they look more casual and primitive and are full of martial bearings endowed by nature. This maybe is the country flavor lost from modern clothes.

The lady dress image of Naxi people in Yunnan Province. (Painted by Li Ling)

A Silhouette of Tibetan Costumes

Age-old Qinghai-Tibet Plateau is where Tibetan, Moinba minority, Lhoba minority etc. live for generations. Majestic Himalayas and wide Brahmaputra River help to bring up their bold and unstrained character and unique clothing culture.

It is hard to generalize Tibetan costumes with just one or two styles of clothes and adornments. For long time, because of Tibet's vast land and inconvenient traffic, Tibetan costumes in different regions are far more difficult to sum up than people expect. On the contrary, Tibetan clothes are of various types, styles and colors.

One of the most typical Tibetan clothes is the Tibetan robe, which is common among people of different sex and age. It has a long robe body. The robe pail is covered with surface cloth with edgings and no pockets and buttons. In daily days, men's robes mostly are plain surface and inlaid with wide black edgings. In festive

A Tibetan young man wearing Tibetan dresses is singing and dancing. (Photo by Ma Fujiang, provided by image library of Hong Kong *Traveling in China*)

< A Tibetan child with many thin plaits. (Photo taken by Wang Miao, provided by image library of Hong Kong *Traveling in China*)

occasions, edgings are colored. Women's robes are more colorful. The material used in the most representative edgings is a kind of wool fabric with delicate colors and patterns. Especially for Tibetan herdsman robe's edgings, they usually use color blocks of blue, green, purple, black, orange and beige color to form a multicolored ribbon. The shoulder, lower hem and cuff of a lady robe are usually decorated with stripes in yellow, red, green and purple of about 10cm. They often use complementary colors, such as red and green, black and white, yellow and purple. Sometimes, they even interweave gold and silver threads inside strong contrasting colors. The bright and harmonious artistic effect displayed by Tibetan robes impresses people deeply.

In places like Tibetan area in Qinghai Province, Gannan area in Gansu Province and Tianzhu and Aba area in Sichuan, men like to use leopard skin as adornments. It is said that this is related with the military life in Tubo Kingdom Period. At that time, tiger skins and leopard skins were used to reward brave soldiers and people with great contributions while fox tails were used to insult dastards and deserters. The typical climate in tableland is cold in morning and evening, but hot in noon, so no matter

(**top**) *The Tibetan women head decorations in Yushu Tibetan area in Qinghai Province.* (Photo by Zhai Dongfeng, provided by image library of Hong Kong *Traveling in China*)
(**middle**) *The Tibetan women dresses in Litang pasturing area in Sichuan Province.* (Photo by Lin Jinghua, provided by image library of Hong Kong *Traveling in China*)
(**bottom**) *A Tibetan young man wearing decorations made by natural precious stones.* (Photo by Xie Guanghui, provided by image library of Hong Kong *Traveling in China*)

men or women, they like to take off the right sleeve and tie it around the waist when weather gets hot in noon. In this way, it could dispel heat, and adjust body temperature. In the past, men bared their body inside robes. Their swarthy and strong arms display the rusticity and sturdiness of the tableland people. Along with the raising of life quality and under the influence of modern city, Tibetan men become accustomed to wear white shirts inside robes in external communication or in festive occasions. Women wear cloth jackets of different small flower patterns inside the robe with one shoulder and arm being exposed outside. This is the kind of typical Tibetan clothes that we are familiar with.

Besides Tibetan robes, there is another kind of typical costume called "Bangdan" in Lhasa, Rikaze area and vast Kangba Area. This is a kind of long apron that is tied around waist and hung from front waist to lower hem of the skirt. The apron is sewn by three separate vertical pieces and on each piece there are colorful horizontal stripes patterns. Also made of wool fabric, this type of apron has horizontal stripes of different width. Scarlet, verdure, blue, lemon yellow, purple and white colors alternate regularly to form the pattern. The apron shines faintly, giving the feel of sunshine.

As for Tibetan hairstyle, some hang down loosely and some make plaits. People in agricultural area mostly do two plaits, while people from pasturing area do multi-plaits. Generally speaking, Tibetan women in many areas hang long hair down to the shoulder.

Tibetan herdsmen under Gangjiaquba Glacier in Qinghai Province. (Photo by Yang Xin, provided by image library of Hong Kong *Traveling in China*)

Head decorations for noble women in the past in Ali area in Tibet. (Photo by Lin Nuhou, provided by image library of Hong Kong *Traveling in China*)

Long hair, faces of suntan, thick eyebrows, big eyes and high noses altogether form a charming image of tableland women. Men nowadays mostly cut hair short. In the past, they wrapped plaits around head top or decorated hair at back with rings made of elephant tooth or ox bone. The primitive wildness shown in their hairstyle is unique to Tibetan tableland.

Adornments are an indispensable part of Tibetan costumes. There are a dazzling variety of adornments including head adornments, ear adornments, chest adornments, waist adornments and finger rings. And materials they use are very rich including gold, silver, pearl, agate, jade, turquoise, silk, emerald, coral, honey wax and amber etc. The most representative one is the "Ba pearl," a kind of triangle or bow shape head adornment. In the past, noble people use pearls or gem stones while common people use coral. The first time a girl starts to wear a Ba pearl, a solemn ritual will be held because it signifies that the girl is a grow-up and ready for marriage. Many beads, silver chains, silver

plates etc. that Tibetan people hang in front of the chest are related with Buddhism. Bead adornments are Buddhist beads. In addition, everyone will wear a talismanic silver Buddhist box to hold the protective Buddhist figure or bodhisattva figure.

Tibetan people usually gird strings of metal knifes, boxes for steel for flint and many other silver adornments around the waist. Among them, broadswords and waist hooks are two kinds of unique adornments for Tibetan men and women. With a long history, Tibetan swords are in different length general from longer than 1 meter to 40-70cm, and some shorter than 40cm. A Tibetan knife or sword has many functions. A long sword could be used for self-protection and a short sword could be used to kill cattle and sheep, to peel off skin and to cut meat and vegetables. A small knife could be used as tableware. Not only very sharp, Tibetan swords are also exquisitely handmade with delicate adornments. The hilt part is covered with ox horn, animal bone or hard wood and then wrapped with silver or copper wires and hoop with bronze hull or iron hull. Some are decorated with silver adornments. The materials used for sheath and the ways of production are also very exquisite. Sheathes are mostly covered with copper or silver and then carved with lucky patterns of dragons, phoenixes, tigers, lions and flowers. Some are covered with sharkskin and inlaid with precious gems such as turquoise, coral and agate. A more common practice is to inlay a piece of yak horn on the knife shank.

Besides girding broadswords, women in Rikaze region also like to carry waist hooks usually made by silver or bronze. The shape of a waist hook is flat and long with both ends in the shape of *ruyi* (an S-shaped ornamental object, usually made of jade, formerly a symbol of good luck) or diamond shape *ruyi*. No matter in what shape, there is a ring under the waist hook, which is not only an ornamental object, but also used to hang things. The patterns on waist hooks not only have motifs of Tibetan Buddhism, such as the treasure bottle, wheel and deer, but also traditional Han motifs such as the phoenix bird, lion and dragon. Among these patterns, there is one called "four brothers getting along well," which originated from a Tibetan folk story. In ancient time, elephants, lions, rabbits and little birds were not able to obtain enough fruits for food due to atrocious weather. Later they united together to work hard, and finally obtained enough fruits. The harvest they obtained is not only material, but also spiritual. Through animal figures and the scene of picking up fruits together, it tells that people should make concerted effort so that they could coexist peaceful.

Though the Moinba and Lhoba minority who also live in Qinghai-Tibetan Plateau have their own languages and costumes, they share many similarities with Tibetan culture as they all live in the south slope of Himalayas, very close to where Tibetan live. Besides wearing similar long robes, Moinba men also wear fur hats, tie waist belts and women also hang hair down loosely or do plaits, wear Buddhist beads and waist hooks. Their boots are also similar to Tibetan boots. But if categorizing carefully, both Moinba costumes and Lhoba costumes have their own special features. For example, both Moinba men and women wear ochre long robes. Men wear brown caps with round crown, orange edge and a small vent in front. They like to wear big earrings and red or black oxhide boots with soft sole. Women wrap white pailform skirts outside their robes and drape cow skin or sheep skin pieces. A kind of head costume unique to Lhoba men, a bear fur hat is mostly a helmet type hat with brims and made through pressing the bear skin. On the brim, people attach a bearskin ring with fur hair extending around. At the back of the hat, there is a piece of trapezifom bear head skin with eye sockets hanging down to the neck, which is said to prevent from being shot by bows or cut by knives. They also attach a bearskin ring with fur under their rattan hoops or round helmets. This kind of hat helmet looks like thick black hair hanging down loosely when looking from a distance, displaying a kind of wild beauty.

Lhoba men and women all like to wear adornments. The adornments that one wears could be as heavy as tens of kilos. Men will tie waist belts, wear silver adornments inlaid with gibbose circle pattern, shells and strings of pearls. Under the belt, they hang several strings of silver beads on both sides. Eardrops they wear are also drooping beads. They hang several rings of necklaces made of different materials in front of the chest. They wear bracelets, gird long swords, carry bows and pipes, cigarette cases and staff like that. The variety of women's adornments is even more astonishing. Turquoise stone necklaces around neck could be more then ten strings or tens of strings. The waist part is full of decorative objects, such as sea shell strings, bronze bells, silver coins, iron chains, copper pieces, steel for flint and little knives. The texture of the material and the quantity of the adornments are closely related with the wearers' financial situations.

Countless Ornamental Objects

The costume culture of Chinese minorities is very colorful, especially those stunning ornamental objects that go with the clothes. Because of the extensive choice of materials, delicate craftsmanship, abundant styles, exquisite patterns and rich connotations, Chinese minorities' ornamental objects are considered to be a rich costume treasury.

Though materials, styles and patterns are different for ornamental objects of all nationalities, the positions on which they wear are about the same, such as the head flower, necklace, earring, bracelet and finger ring. Besides these adornments that they all like to wear, every nationality has its unique adornments with unique cultural connotations and ways of wearing.

Traditional Han women like to decorate their hair with flowers and all kinds of earrings. This is the New Year picture A Beautiful Lady Holding a Fan. (Collected by Wang Shucun)

140

Pictures of all earrings on this page were taken by Chen Xiaolong.

Sometimes, the adornments are more symbolic than clothes or contain more national cultural contents. They are all narrating their national history in a unique way and recording the glory and dream of their nationality.

People are dazzled and fascinated by the affection that Tu minority people show toward colors and the audacity and enthusiasm that they show in the use of colors. They like to use orange, ginger yellow, verdure, dark green, sky blue, light blue, scarlet, pink, blue and white. Tu women attach great importance to their head adornments, which were called "niuda" by local people call. In the past, the style of "niuda" differed in different places, but it gradually formed into one style when entering the modern time only with the difference between married women and the unmarried. Girls usually do three plaits and married women do double plaits. The ends of plaits are connected and decorated with coral, turquoise and trumpet shell pieces. Tu women usually wear gold, silver or copper earrings decorated with red coral and emerald and carved with patterns. Colorful beads with tassels hang down from earrings. Among them the most beautiful one is the silver eardrops – using colorful porcelain bead strings to connect the earrings. Like several necklaces, the bead strands hang down in front of the chest. Tu women wear neck rings inlaid with more than twenty seashell pieces and hang patterned purses, pouches, small copper bells and

colorful silk tassels around waist.

Yugur women will start to wear *tou mian* when they become adults, which show that they are ready for participating in social activities and marriage. The most representative Yugur ornament, *tou mian* is an indispensable part in festive occasions when women need to dress up.

The way to wear is that first do the hair in three plaits at the left, right and behind, and then use three *tou mians* inlaid with silver plates, coral, agate, pearls, shells to tie around the three plaits. With a usual weight of 3.5 kg, a *tou mian* is divided into three segments connected by metal rings. The *tou mian* starts at the earring position and its length is decided by the body height. Head adornments for girls are also characteristic. The upper part of a long red cloth ribbon is decorated with coral beads of all different colors and the lower edge is decorated with tassels woven by coral

(**top**) *Head decorations for women of Hani minority in Xishuangbanna in Yunnan Province.* (Photo by Chen Yinian, provided by image library of Hong Kong *Traveling in China*)

(**bottom**) *The dress and adornment for women of Dong minority in Guizhou Province.* (Photo by Lu Xianyi, provided by image library of Hong Kong *Traveling in China*)

beads of red, yellow, white, green, blue and jade stones. These decorative ribbons hang down to the eyebrow in front of the forehead like a bead curtain.

Kazakstan women also like to hang a bead curtain in front of the forehead, not as a separate head adornment, but a pendant from the hat. This kind of hat is the symbol of the bride. Unmarried women use hard shell round pipe shape small hats sewn by red, green or yellow flannelette. The hat crown is embroidered with gold threads and decorated with an owl feather. Kazakstan people believe that owl feathers signify courage and steadiness, so they like to use them as a kind of decoration. There is another kind of round hat made of silk, satin, cotton cloth and otter or lambskin. It is embroidered with flower patterns on top of hat crown and inlaid with beads, agate and plugholes made of gold and silver where an owl feather is plug in.

Lisu women's adornments are different in different living places. For example, married Lisu women who live in the Nu river area in Yunnan wear big bronze rings or silver rings that hang down to shoulders, head adornments called "Ele" stringed by tridacna shell pieces, and hang adornments made of beads of different colors and agate in front of the chest. Lisu women in Lijiang area like to wrap cloth head covers decorated with beads and hang necklaces made by beads. Lisu girls in Dehong region wear red, white, or yellow handkerchiefs fully decorated with beads. Silver bells, silver bulbs and beads pendants hang down from the handkerchiefs and the end of pendants are decorated with colorful pompons and tassels. They wear silver neck rings, silver ornamental locks connected by bead strings and several or dozens of necklaces.

There is a beautiful legend about "Ele," the typical adornment to Lisu women. Long long ago, a beautiful girl and a handsome young fellow fell in love. The young man hunted in remote mountains and wild forests all day long. His body was severely hurt by tree twigs because he had no clothes to put on. The young girl felt very sad after seeing this, so she crossed mountains and found some wild linen. She peeled off the fiber from the linen skin, and twisted threads. She spent many days and nights and finally wove threads into cloth. With the cloth, she made clothes and gave them to the young men. With a wish that the girl would look more beautiful, the young man then gave the girl an " ele" that he wove by coral beads. Since then, the "ele" has become a kind of head adornment for the girls and a keepsake between Lisu young men and women.

Jingpo women's silver adornments are very striking. If a young Jingpo woman

(**top**) *The exquisite wrist adornments and finger rings for Mongolian women.* (Photo by Shan Xiaogang, provided by image library of Hong Kong *Traveling in China*)

(**middle**) *A lady of Dai minority covered by silver adornments.* (Photo by Li Zhixiong, provided by image library of Hong Kong *Traveling in China*)

(**bottom**) *The decorations worn in holidays for Niru people in Yunnan Province.* (Photo by Cao Guozhong, provided by image library of Hong Kong *Traveling in China*)

walks toward us from a distance, the first thing that will attract us is the shining silver adornments in front of the chest. Because they like to wear black round-neck short jackets, silver ornaments look especially dazzling. Besides chest adornments, they also hang several silver necklaces and silver rings. These ornaments not only look shining, but also clang when they walk. Together with the scarlet pailform skirts and scarlet hair hoops usually wore by women, the arrangement of black, white and red color complementing each other creates a striking artistic effect.

Women of Nu minority also wear chest adornments, mostly bead strands made by coral, agate, shells, beads, silver coins. The color alternates among red, green and white. Some wear head adornments made by red beads strands, or wrap red rattan around the head. Besides, they like to pierce through ears with bamboo pipes or wear big copper earrings. Though materials used share some similarities with other nationalities, there is something new and fresh in the process of making and ornamental effect displayed.

In terms of adornments, the nationality that has the largest amount of adornments should be Miao minority whose adornments are almost all made of silver. It is fair to say that Miao's silver adornments are the most outstanding among all nationalities. Whenever women need to dress up, they must wear silver adornments. There are a big variety of types including silver hair pins, silver cattle horns, silver hats, silver combs, silver fans, silver neck rings, silver earrings, silver shawls, silver chest locks, silver waist chains, silver bells, silver bracelets and silver finger rings etc.. A Miao lady who is in full dress might wear silver adornments as heavy

Most of the adornments of Gejia women in Guizhou are made of silver. For full dress, they wear necklaces made of natural stones going with silver neck rings. (Photo by Chen Yinian, provided by image library of Hong Kong *Traveling in China*)

as 10 to 15 kilos. Miao people believe that wearing silver adornments is not just to show their wealth or for the aesthetic needs, most important it is to pray for luckiness and drive the evils away.

Miao people have a long history and high-level craftsmanship in making silver ornaments. There is a rich variety in designs and patterns, such as the silver bracelet, silver ring, hollow, solid wood shaving shape, hexagonal and column styles. Among Miao's silver adornments, the ox horn style head adornment is the most stunning and representative one. This kind of silver ox horn adornment is very popular in Southeast regions of Guizhou. Women who are in full dress will plug in a silver ox horn in their tall hair chignon. A silver ox horn is made of white silver pieces of different thickness with the two corners turning up. Like a water buffalo horn, it is about 1 meter if adding the height

146

Some handed down folk belt adornments.
(Photo by Lu Zhongmin)

and width and weighs one kilo. The ox horn is decorated with flower patterned silver fans.

There is another kind of wooden ox horn head adornment, mainly popular in Miao living regions in Guizhou such as Guiyang and Bijie. This kind of ox horn ornament is made by wood, about 50cm long with two horns turning up and comb dents in the middle to wrap and secure the hairpiece. Women first coil up their long hair around head top, and then secure the wooden ox horn ornament to the head top with hairpiece and black cotton threads or silk threads. The reason why this kind of ornament imitates ox horn is because of primitive worship. Miao people worship cattle and consider them as sacred cattle from heaven that are sent to human world to help people furrow and plough and bring happiness to the human world. So they would celebrate birthday for the cattle every year and

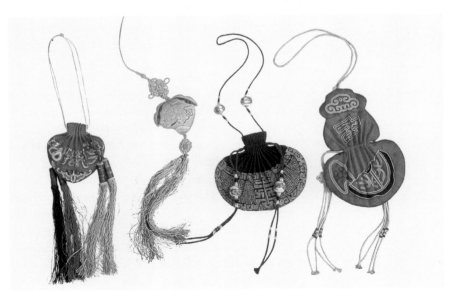

Decorative pouches are a kind of belt adornment used by both men and women which were spread to rather wide areas in China. (Photo by Lu Zhongmin)

hold sacrifice ritual to respect and worship the oxen. It is said among people that in ancient time, Miao men moved to their wife's family after getting married. In order to dress up the bridegroom and make him look masculine and strong, people would put on a pair of wooden ox horns on top of the head. Besides dressing up the bridegroom, making the wedding more extravagant, the ox horn ornament is also for the purpose of warding off the evils. In modern time, wedding tradition changes into women moving to their husbands' home after getting married, so the ox horn head adornment now becomes the bride's ornament. Till today, the ornament is not limited to wedding occasions and has become part of Miao's festive costumes. Besides using large amount of silver adornments, Miao's embroidered clothes are also very delicate. For example, on a bride's embroidered jacket, the number of decorative triangles folded by yellow pieces could reach 17,000. Girls start to make these decorative triangles when they are six or seven years old. When these girls finally finish making their bride jacket with great efforts, they are about to reach the age to get married. Adornments accompany the whole life of Miao women.

People of Dong minority also like silver adornments. They attach great importance to the quantity and delicacy of the adornments. For Dong women's full dress, there are dozens of head adornments such as the silver flowers, silver hats, silver chest adornments, silver neck rings and silver bracelets etc. Some of the hanging chains are twist style and some are connecting rings style. For the silver

All jewelries on this page are provided by Gao Chunming.

Women of Jino minority in Xishuangbanna in Yunnan Province wearing full holiday dresses. (Photo by Guo Jianshe, provided by image library of Hong Kong *Traveling in China*)

ornamental hat, there are 18 arhats inlaid on the top layer, 18 plum blossoms on the lower layer and two male lions on both temple parts of the brim. The ornamental object shows not only Dong's exquisite craftsmanship but also their wish for luckiness. After a woman gives birth to a child, her family will give the grandson silver adornments as presents including silver hats, silver locks, silver neck rings, and silver bracelets. Dong women like to wear clothes of simple and plain color. Mainly using black, blue, purple and white as the base color, they only use light green or light rose pink color when they need to do embroidery on some parts, which is similar to Shui national costumes. Shui people also like to wear black or blue jackets and silver chest locks, silver neck rings, silver bracelets, silver earrings, silver waist chains, silver combs and silver buttons etc.

The most well-known Maonan costume is the patterned bamboo hat. Its main function is not to shelter sunshine and rain, but mostly as a kind of adornment. In most occasions, it is used as the keepsake between lovers. The patterned bamboo hat is decorated by silver adornments, such as a hairpin, silver comb, and silver ring. The silver neck rings, silver kylins, silver plates or silver buttons adorns the outside of their black or blue clothes.

Li women who live in Hainan Island also cover their body with silver adornments including silver hairpins, silver bells in front of chest, silver neck rings, hanging silver plates, silver waist chains and silver foot rings. There are silver adornments arranged orderly even on the lower hem of the clothes. Not limited to silver ornaments, Li women also love neck rings made of copper coins, red cloth pendants, steel waist swords and bead ornamental strings made of beads of different colors. Even the gun carrying bag and power bag are all embroidered with colorful patterns.

Comparably speaking, Gaoshan people who live in Taiwan Island, even till the modern time, still keep many adornments that contain primitive meaning, which well document human being's childhood fun. For example, the shell adornments, glass beads, pig teeth, bear teeth, feathers, animal skin pieces, flowers, copper or silver adornments, ornamental coins or bones, silver buttons and bamboo pipes. Gaoshan Taiya people have a kind of very precious costume. They polish the shell pieces carefully and make them into small beads with holes. Then these beads were stringed with thin linen threads and sewn onto the clothes in rows. It is said that at least fifty to sixty thousand shell beads are needed to make such a bead coat.

It is hard to describe minority's adornments in just several pages of paper. Since 1980s, along with the reform and the open door policy, young people of minorities one after another walk out of the remote mountains and valley into cities. Some adornments have shown a tendency to die out. The Han people's clothes are experiencing a tendency of westernization while minorities' costumes get Hanzified quickly. Facing the impact of the modern social industrialization, will these handicrafts made with heart and soul gradually die out?

Silver accouterments have a long history in China. This kind of silver decorative lock carrying the best wish of longevity and luckiness is still a folk tradition that had been handed down for generations. (Photo by Lu Zhongmin)

Keeping Pace with the World Fashion

In 1978, China started to reform and adopted the open door policy. Since then, fashion and fashion culture have entered common Chinese people's life. As a part of western culture, a series of fashionable western garments, like the continuous wind, are changing the image of Chinese costumes gradually. Since the end of 1970s, besides asking tailors to make their clothes, people have started to purchase ready-made clothes. Clothes processing industry developed quickly along with the open door policy and reform. There are more and more clothes brands, design and colors in the market. People believe more and more in the quality and taste represented by the brand clothes. Taking examples of several types of popular clothes, it is not difficult to see how Chinese blend in the world fashion in dressing.

Bell pants are also called bell-bottomed pants. This kind of trousers has short crotch, thin and tight cut in

The picture shows a performing stage built according to the traditional Chinese architectural style. The theme of the fashion show was "dialogue between the tradition and the modern". (Provided by Imaginechina)

In hot summer in 1979, at the beginning of China's opening door and reform, a diversified fashion trend appeared in Chinese streets instead of the drab solitary dressing image. (Photographed in 1979, provided by Xinhua News Agency photo department)

hip and thigh part. From the knee part, the legs of trousers are widened and loosened, making the trousers look like bell shape. Originally it was a kind of sailor clothes. Loosening the trousers legs was to cover the rubber boots, which was to prevent seawater or deck cleaning water being poured into the boots. Bell-bottomed trousers originally were American decadent style clothes, popular from the end of 1960s to the end of 1970s. In 1978, it was about the end of bell-bottomed pants' popularity in Europe and America when China opened its door to outside world. Bell-bottomed trousers became popular among young people in China overnight and then were quickly spread to the whole country. Jackets go with them are tight elastic jackets, displaying an "A" shape.

Together with bell-bottomed pants, sunglasses also entered into China. As early as in 1930s, "dark glasses" were once very popular in big cities in China. Made of citrines or smoky quartz, the spectacle lens of dark glasses are small and in round shape. Dark glasses were once very popular among fashionable people. At the end of 1970s, sunglasses entered China again, but the popular styles were "toad style" and "panda style." The spectacle lenses are big and in the shape of toad or panda bear. One of the fashionable ways was to wear the sunglasses on top of the head or hang in front of the chest. Many young men, due to their worship for foreign things, even kept the brand stick paper on the glasses on purpose in order to show that their glasses were a foreign product. Since then, the styles of sunglasses have experienced constant changes. Chinese followed closely with the world glasses fashion.

Jeans also entered into China at the end of 1970s. And since then, more and more people have started to wear jeans, expanding from fashionable young men to people of all classes and ages. In 1990s, types of jeans developed including short skirts, short pants, waistcoats, jackets, hats, satchels, and backpacks. Colors were not limited to blue. New materials appeared such as water washing thin materials. At the beginning of 1980s, bat clothes were very popular. This type of clothes look like bat wings when stretching the two sleeves. With various types of collars, a bat pullover's sleeves and clothes body integrate into a whole. There are no sewing threads on the sleeves. The lower hem of the pullover is tight. Later more types were developed such as the bat coats, bat overcoats and bat jackets etc. It is quite interesting that this clothes style re-appeared in 2004 spring and summer fashion trend as a kind of retro.

Till the middle term of 1980s, there were more and more clothes styles while the popularity circle became shorter and shorter. New styles and materials were kept being introduced to the market. As for upper outer garments, there were all kinds of T-shirts, jackets of mixing color, checkered shirts and cotton pullovers. Wearing suits and ties became social dresses for formal occasions, and accepted by most of the white collars. Under clothes included pailform trousers, elastic trousers, radish trousers, skirt trousers, 70% trousers, trousers skirts, pleated skirts, eight-piece skirts, western suits skirts, midis and sun skirts. The style changed constantly. By the time when the mini skirt that was born in the western world in 1960s was once again popular in 1980s, China has kept pace with the world fashion.

At the beginning of 1990s, the previous dressing order was broken. The sweaters worn inside the jacket in the past entered all kinds of formal occasions as a single dress without going with outer jackets because of their rather loose style. The dressing style of "wearing underwear outside" was not considered as strange any more after two or three years. In the past, if wearing a jacket outside, the sweater or T-shirts inside should be shorter than the jacket. But young people suddenly found that it was hard to find bigger jackets than their loose sweaters, so they covered small jackets outside the long sweaters. The short-sleeve sweaters worn in summer time could also be worn outside the long-sleeve shirts. Very soon, clothes industry began to launch sets of unconventional suits, such as a long jacket and long shirt going with a little waistcoat higher than waist, or the successive style sleeves with outer sleeves shorter than the underclothes sleeves.

During that period of time, sun skirts going with high boots style black satin saddle shoes appeared in Paris garments stage. In the past, sun skirts with tight and small upper skirt part and two thin shoulder straps were worn in beach. But when it appeared in fashion stage, the skirt body had a bigger spread that reached the ankles. Almost at the same time, global fashion experienced first hand-covering clothes, which lengthened sleeves to cover the hands, then the waist-exposing clothes or even navel-

The Chinese version of Elle *magazine started publication in 1998, which became the first international magazine published in mainland China with the official approval.* (Provided by Imaginechina)

Central cities in all over China all have large scale shopping centers with advanced facilities. (Provided by Imaginechina)

exposing clothes, which have short and small upper clothes and a section of skin exposed. This kind of clothes was once popular in China, but the style was not as bold as the neighboring Japan. The navel-exposing clothes popular in Japan even led to a new content of body beautification- to beautify the navel. Clothes that expose part of skin inspired by waist-exposing or navel-exposing clothes however became popular in China. A subtle trend was to cover parts that were exposed before such as hands and shanks and expose parts that were covered before such as the waist and navel. The sandal shoes without back support was once the rage. Women wore the sandal shoes barefoot, painted nail polish, glued decorative plastic pieces or wore toe rings. Designers even

Chinese young people understand the latest international fashion trend and dare to show off. (Photo by Xie Guanghui, provided by image library of Hong Kong Traveling in China)

156

designed the transparent handbag or watches that expose mechanism in order to show the open concept of modern people.

It was from 1990s that many oversea famous brand costumes one after another aimed at Chinese consumer market and opened the monopolization stores in big cities such as Beijing, Shanghai, Shenzhen and Guangzhou. Domestic Chinese brand clothes and fashion models gradually attracted people's interests. Along with the first fashion magazine that used foreign copyrights coming into being in China in 1988, more and more newspaper, magazines, radio stations, television stations and networks entered the fashion promotion field. World latest fashion information could be introduced to China very quickly. The trend of garments in fashion, hairstyles and make-up styles from France, Italy, U.K and South Korea directly influence the trend in China. Life styles and dressing styles represented by "fashion" are accepted and went after by more and more Chinese.

In those years at the turn of century, fashion in China kept close pace with the world fashion. Following the international dressing fashion, dressing style tended to be more formal, especially white-collar women who paid particular attention to the charm of being a professional woman. They tried to wear formal and decent

A cosmetic counter opened in China by the well-known cosmetic brand DIOR. (Photo by Shen Yi, provided by Imaginechina)

dresses. People no longer favored the so-called "original wildness," such as no edging for the straw hats or tearing thread off the trousers. The trend of exposing certain part of skin was restrained among people of some classes and in some occasions. Though mini skirts were still popular, many young girls started to favor ankle-long long skirts to show the female elegance.

Of course, some adolescent young boys and girls who advocated the anti-tradition consciousness of the western society considered the weird as fashionable on purpose, for example, imitating the hairstyle of *The Last of the Mohicans* to shave head on two sides and leave the middle section and dye hair. Some wore "punk dress" – another kind of decadent style youth dress in western society after hippies. They glued the hair into animal horn shape using hair gel and embroidered skeleton pattern on black leather jackets; or intentionally tore or burned holes on the clothes. These were not dominant in China fashion scene. But

In 2002, models who participated in New Silk Road Chinese Models Competition were taking photos in beautiful Sanya beaches of Hainan Island, showing their charming glamour. (Photo by Mao Jianjun, provided by Imaginechina)

a very interesting fact was that "opening a window" in an artistic way on clothes became popular at the turn of spring and summer in 1998. Holes could be dug in every part of the clothes and the edge of holes was dealt with carefully. As this style of clothes was different from the "transparent dress" made by translucent materials, it was called the "perspective dress." And then a kind of dress full of mesh appeared, which was synchronous with the "fishnet" dress in the Paris fashion stage.

In those several years, a "swimming suit trend" emerged in streets and lanes in China. Of course, the swimming suit here didn't mean the swimming suit for the water sport sold in the shop, but a kind of daily dress. It got this name because the suit was as short, small and sexy as the swimming suit. Imagine that a girl wears a tight upper dress that exposes the navel and with thin shoulder straps, a mini short skirt or short pants and a pair of slippers, one will easily think she is beside the beach or swimming pool but not in the streets of the city if not for the backpack she carries.

At the beginning of 21st century, adult women including young ladies and university students fell over themselves for child style clothes and hairstyles as if they wanted to relive their childhood. They cut a kind of kid hairstyle, which was to curl the tip of hair on both temples, and put on pink or lemon yellow butterfly or flower hairpins. The upper clothes sometime were tight and small and sometimes loose and cute, which made them look like naughty kids. They wore kids style shoes with square openings and slanting shoelaces and carried satchels with patterns of bear head. Some students, like kids who refused to grow up, even hung rubber nipples or mobile phones in front of the chest.

In 2001, the small Chinese belly-cover was once very popular. In the awarding ceremony of Cannes Film Festival, the movie star Zhang Ziyi attracted the attention of the fashion circle when she wore a specially made red belly cover, and draped a long piece of red silk around shoulder, which made her look like an ancient Chinese doll. Later, wearing a diamond shape belly-cover without any additional adornments, she appeared in the MTV awarding ceremony. So very soon, in all kinds of occasions and media formats, no matter stars or ordinary fashionable girls all began to wear all kinds of belly covers.

At the beginning of the 21st century, there was also a big change on the shoe vamp. In 2002, those cute "sponge cake" shoes were no longer popular while shoes with sharp turning up tips (like Charlie Chaplin style shoes) and decorated with shining adornments appeared. One year after, round tip style shoes that imitated the toe shoes were the rage in the market.

At the end of 20th century, international fashion world began to favor oriental style. Oriental elegance, tranquility, simplicity and mystery became the global fashion elements. With the rising of China's position in the world, overseas Chinese started to feel proud to wear Chinese costumes, women in Mainland China naturally put on Chinese jackets and many Chinese men consider Chinese cotton jackets as fashionable. Chinese dresses of nowadays are not like those classical traditional Chinese coats or jackets. Many female Chinese costumes adopted the fashionable elements. The costume arrangement looks rather interesting when girls put on print or flamboyant cotton cloth coats with edgings and stand collar, jeans and leather shoes in the latest fashion.

Traditional Chinese dress shops offer custom made service and sell expensive Chinese style dresses. (Provided by Imaginechina)

At the beginning of 2001, Hong Kong movie *In the Mood for Love* was played in many countries domestic and abroad. The actress in the movie changed cheong-sams of different colors and styles (more than 20) under the dark lights. Audiences were amazed by the classical charm of the oriental beauty. The actress looked beautiful, elegant and sentimental with cheong-sams. People for the first time found that Chinese traditional dresses had a kind of special charm. Due to the magic of the movie, the cheong-sam once again was the rage.

Western style wedding dresses have become trendy among city brides and many new couples like to take wedding photos in parks. (Photo by Liang Zhen, provided by Imaginechina)

160

Knowing fashion and leading fashion become a lifestyle advocated by many city young people. (Photo by Chen Shu, provided by Imaginechina)

Nobody would expect that APEC conference held in China – a very influential political activity, created another round of Chinese dress fashion. In autumn 2001 in Shanghai, the whole world was stirred when leaders from all countries who put on Chinese blue, red or green satin jackets appeared in the public. International media published the photos of the leaders wearing Chinese dresses and wrote articles with comments. The charm of Chinese "button in the middle" style jacket coupling with the huge effect created by Bush and Putin made a very successful advertisement for the Chinese costume. Some customers asked the shop assistant to give them a "Putin" style Chinese jacket. Another background behind this trend is the more and more important influence that China has on the world stage. The Chinese dress rage also signifies the constantly increased confidence and cohesion of the Chinese nation.

What happened in the 20th century has proved that this century is till now the most fashionable century with high amount of clothes, accessories and cosmetics being sold. The development of the increasingly powerful media makes more and more people to come close, to appreciate clothes and to enjoy the beauty of the fashionable garments. Fashionable garments have become a kind of life style that people understand and love to invest.